# Overcoming Loneliness in Everyday Life

# Overcoming Loneliness in Everyday Life

Jacqueline Olds, M.D.
Richard S. Schwartz, M.D.
Harriet Webster

A BIRCH LANE PRESS BOOK
Published by Carol Publishing Group

For our children, Nate and Sarabeth, without whom this book never would have been written.

Jacqueline Olds
Richard S. Schwartz

For Charlie, my dearest friend.

Harriet Webster

Copyright © 1996 Jacqueline Olds, Richard S. Schwartz, Harriet Webster

A Birch Lane Press Book
Published by Carol Publishing Group
Birch Lane Press is a registered trademark of Carol Communications, Inc.
Editorial Offices: 600 Madison Avenue, New York, N.Y. 10022
Sales and Distribution Offices: 120 Enterprise Avenue, Secaucus, N.J. 07094
In Canada: Canadian Manda Group, One Atlantic Avenue, Suite 105,
    Toronto, Ontario M6K 3E7
Queries regarding rights and permissions should be addressed to Carol
Publishing Group, 600 Madison Avenue, New York, N.Y. 10022

Carol Publishing Group books are available at special discount for bulk purchases, sales promotion, fund-raising, or educational purposes. Special editions can be created to specifications. For details, contact: Special Sales Department, Carol Publishing Group, 120 Enterprise Avenue, Secaucus, N.J. 07094

Manufactured in the United States of America
10  9  8  7  6  5  4  3  2  1

Library of Congress Cataloging-in-Publication Data

Olds, Jacqueline.
    Overcoming loneliness in everyday life / Jacqueline Olds, Richard
Schwartz, and Harriet Webster.
        p.    c.m
    "A Birch Lane Press book."
    ISBN 1-55972-343-2
    1. Loneliness.   2. Individualism.   3. Adjustment (Psychology)
I. Schwartz, Richard (Richard S.)   II. Webster, Harriet.   III. Title.
BF575.L7024   1996
158'.2—dc20                                    95-47097
                                               CIP

# Contents

# Acknowledgments

We have depended heavily on the kindness of family, friends, and colleagues in writing this book. Some of the ideas that led to it emerged from intertwined lives in Cambridge where we shared childrearing and emotional support with four families: the Lyne-McSweeneys, the Weeds, the Slywotzkys, and the Flemings. Early support for this book came from Kate Flora, Maggie and Craig McEwen, Jo Solet, Marion Dry, and our agent Caroline Krupp. Susan Leland, James Olds, Doris and Stephen Schwartz, and Adrian Slywotzky offered supportive responses to various drafts. Ken Cohen and Barbara Herzstein very generously provided detailed critical readings. Professor Pauline Maier was extremely helpful in directing us to historical material relevant to the hypotheses in chapter two. Nancy and Hubert Murray were generous with their time and good advice through all stages of the project. Hillel Black, our editor and publisher, sustained us with an astute mix of enthusiasm and realism. And finally, many thanks to our children, Nate and Sarabeth, for their wisdom, kindness, and patience throughout the process of writing this book.

Jacqueline Olds
Richard S. Schwartz

I would like to thank my agent, Julian Bach, for the insight, support, and kindness he has shown me over the past ten years. I am grateful to his colleague, Carolyn Krupp, for her tenacity and good will. My neighbors Dick Prouty and David Cohen helped me understand the nature of small groups and my friend Sandy Ronan has opened my ideas to new ways of thinking about the role of community in midlife and later. I appreciate their contributions, as well as those of the members of my writers' group; we've been hashing out ideas together for thirteen years.

And, as always, I am grateful to my children—David, Matt, and Ben Webster—for their enduring tolerance and good humor.

Harriet Webster

# Authors to Reader

"Don't use the word *loneliness* in your title. No one will buy the book." This advice came to us from a knowledgeable source and it intrigued us.

The results of a recent Gallup Poll indicate that over 36 percent of Americans acknowledge recent feelings of loneliness. Working as psychiatrists over a period of twenty years, we have discovered that loneliness is one of the chief sources of unhappiness in our patients' lives. Furthermore, new medical research demonstrates that loneliness has negative effects on our physical health. Yet the marketing advice sounded right. Why, we wondered, would people avoid buying a book about loneliness?

We think the answer lies in the shame that most people feel when they are lonely. An admission of loneliness seems to transform us into exactly the kind of people no one would want to be with anyway. Thus loneliness appears to condemn us to even more loneliness. Better to keep any books with that unpleasant word on the cover safely out of the house and get on with the job of presenting ourselves as happily sociable, or at least content in our solitude. Then someone might actually want to be with us.

In the first section of the book, we explore the problem of loneliness by examining the roots of a distinctly American culture that prizes self-sufficiency above all else and has a particular distaste for anything that smacks of dependency. These are the values behind such oft-repeated phrases as "Thanks anyway, but I can take care of it myself" and "I wouldn't consider imposing on him." We believe that a better understanding of the historical development of these cultural values can help us figure out how we get ourselves into isolated corners and how we can go about escaping them.

In this section we also examine a rapidly expanding body of medical research that suggests a biological need for social connections. In exploring the effects of social isolation on our physical and psychological well-being, we find evidence that people with a rich social network tend to live longer, suffer less from illnesses as diverse as heart disease and depression, have better functioning immune systems, and are less likely to commit abuse within the family than their more lonely counterparts.

The second section rounds out our cultural perspective with a look at the three major ways in which our society has attempted to solve the problem of isolation: psychotherapy, medication, and self-help groups.

In the third section of the book we shift to a more informal style as we focus on the practical aspects of creating a social network in everyday life. While seeing a psychotherapist may solve the problem of loneliness in the short term, it does not always address the issue of how to get hooked into a social web that will provide long-term protection against loneliness and its consequences. Today it is fashionable to seek psychotherapy to alleviate feelings of low self-esteem. We suspect that for many people, worries about low self-esteem actually provide a socially acceptable route to getting help in dealing with their loneliness and the enormous shame and unhappiness it provokes in them.

Several years ago we conducted a research study to examine the effect of different child care arrangements on marriage. Through this study, we came to appreciate the strength of the "natural forces" that can so easily push a couple down diverging paths. If left untended, these natural forces can make marriage itself seem lonely. We came to appreciate how much married couples need a joint endeavor in their lives (like truly shared parenting of their children) to keep their relationship vital over the long haul. We realized then that a shared endeavor leading to mutual interdependence and deeper relationships was a simple, even obvious, solution to the more general problem of loneliness that we encountered so frequently in our work as therapists. But if the solution was so obvious, we asked ourselves, why are so many people still so helpless when it comes to doing something to ease their loneliness?

Part of the answer lies in our collective embarrassment about loneliness. Convinced that being open about our loneliness will only repel the very people with whom we would like to connect, we struggle to keep up the pretense of needing no one. But in doing so, we miss the boat. Our clinical and research experience has instead convinced us that when we take the risk of asking for help, we open the door to a pattern of give and take that propels us out of loneliness and into the mesh of a social network.

Throughout our discussion, we describe the experiences of people who take on shared projects or joint tasks and discover that their cooperative effort leads to the unexpected bonus of cultivating a context in which their relationships can deepen. The stories are drawn from the lives of friends, patients, couples in our child care study, and our own lives. They illustrate the effects of shared tasks in a variety of situations including marriage, family, neighborhood, and living alone. We find that when a mutual task involves a process of give and take, that when two individuals allow themselves to help and be helped with grace and good will, it creates a powerful ripple effect in their lives. Their "relevance" to each other develops at a pace which is natural and fruitful, rather than contrived. They discover, over time, that their lives have become entwined.

We show how these shared tasks have fallen out of favor in a country that, paradoxically, was built by community effort despite its historical regard for self-sufficiency. As people become more established today, they feel reluctant to impose on others by asking even the smallest favors. Instead of arranging a neighborhood baby-sitting cooperative, a lonely young mother hires a housekeeper. She manages to secure the free time she needs, but her solution does nothing to ease her loneliness. Yet when someone is tied to others through the interdependence of mutual tasks, loneliness is reduced and self-esteem grows.

The concept of shared tasks is deceptively simple, but it is crucial to an understanding of how relationships actually develop and deepen in everyday life. We show how a self-sufficient refusal to share responsibilities and to depend on others can place the lives of otherwise caring individuals on separate trajectories that stray farther and farther apart over time. The range of our examples makes clear how a shared task creates a setting in which regular contact insures the deepening of relationships. Once we have come to grips with our cultural bias against leaning on one another, we can begin to appreciate the simplicity and naturalness of shared tasks and apply that concept to our own lives.

In the final section of the book, we attempt to weave together the major themes introduced earlier on. All of us, of course, need time for solitude. A frenetic social life is no closer to our ideal than a life shut off from the vitality of others. We need to create a comfortable balance. We hope this book will help you find that balance, first by easing the shame which acts as a barrier to overcoming loneliness and then by offering specific strategies for building a strong social network.

# Part I
# The Problem

# 1   Our Increasing Isolation

It is late afternoon on a warm, spring weekday. Cut off from the sounds of the street by the music that courses through his headset, a lone male runner passes through the middle-class suburban neighborhood. On another block, a young mother pushes her toddler's stroller down the empty sidewalk. Later on, a man walks by with a dog on a leash. Otherwise, the street, sidewalks, yards, and driveways remain silent and lifeless, interrupted only when someone hustles between house and car.

Sadly, this scene is typical of even the safest neighborhoods. Seldom do we see a group of children playing together in the street or jumping rope in a driveway. It is rare to come upon a cluster of mothers hanging out together in the park, watching their youngsters play. When we do encounter such a scene, it fills us with nostalgia. More often today, the mothers and fathers are working, and the children are safely enrolled in day care or recreational programs. It seems that the runner with earphones is emblematic of our time: We listen to our own music and do "our own thing" by ourselves when it best fits our schedule.

In inner city neighborhoods, residents isolate themselves for different reasons. Mothers fear their children will be caught in a drive-by shooting or seduced by the drug–gun culture. They keep their children indoors to protect them from harm. Adults also fear being caught in a random wave of violence. They pick up the evening newspaper on the way home from work instead of going out for it in the evening, anxious to lock themselves inside their apartments before dark falls. So individuals and families hunker down with their televisions and video games, keeping safe while watching the dangerous world unfold on TV programs produced to feed their fears.

Social scientists report that Americans feel more lonely and less trusting than ever before. As previously noted, in a national survey 36 percent of the respondents said they have recently felt lonely.[1] In addition, the proportion of Americans who feel most people can be trusted has decreased from 58 percent in 1960 to 37 percent in 1993. Meanwhile, U.S. Census statistics show that we are increasingly less likely to share our homes. In 1950, 10.8 percent of households consisted of one person living alone; forty-five years later, that figure has risen to 25.1 percent.[2] This increase reflects changes in our family constellations. The proportion of adults who have not married has increased from 28 percent in 1970 to 41 percent today. *The Lifestyle Odyssey* reports that "as many as 60 percent of today's children under ten years old will live with one parent for a time with almost one-third living with a parent who was never married."[3,4,5]

Robert Putnam, a researcher at Harvard University, has observed that Americans are less likely today to join civic associations than ever before. When he looked at church groups, school related groups (like PTAs), labor unions, fraternal organizations, traditional women's clubs, and political groups, he found that all have experienced a serious decline in participation despite the increase in average level of education reflected across the population. This reluctance to join associations is mirrored in our national voting record. Americans are far less likely to vote today than in the early 1960s (voter turnout has declined by 25 percent since then).[6] Thus, not only is a greater percentage of the population going about their lives alone, but this fact seems to lead to an increasing reluctance to participate in our democracy.

These statistics raise many questions: What happened to the sense of social connectedness that helped America become a generous, friendly country to live in? Is loneliness more pervasive today than in former eras? Ought we to recognize it as a problem of our culture rather than simply a problem afflicting individuals? If loneliness is indeed more widespread, and we think it is, what has caused this expansion and what are the consequences for individuals, families, and our nation as a whole? Lastly, what can we as individuals do to turn the tide on the epidemic of loneliness?

We believe that there are certain values concerning independence and individualism implicit in our culture that have made this epidemic nearly inevitable in spite of the cost it imposes on families and individuals and on the greater society.

Specifically, we contend that our national tendency to glorify independence and our collective wish to appear self-sufficient maneuver us toward a position of pseudoindependence as we become more affluent. This position leaves us feeling so lonely that it diminishes our sense of self and our sense of connection with others. As well as making us unhappy, a false sense of independence also affects our physical well-being.

In the pages that follow, we examine an impressive body of new medical research that relates loneliness and social isolation to a variety of illnesses and even increased mortality rates. In addition, we discuss other factors contributing to the erosion of a sense of community in our country. Most important, we discuss ways of creating common ground, which can provide a setting for the germination and growth of satisfying and enduring relationships.

People who experience a sense of loneliness often feel depressed. Statistics tell us that depression is on the rise in our society. The number of people who use antidepressant medication to alleviate symptoms of depression continues to increase. They use the drugs to improve their outlook and relieve their pain. (Perhaps part of the enormous success of Peter Kramer's *Listening to Prozac* can be attributed to the curiosity of the large number of patients for whom the drug has been prescribed.) Feeling isolated can be both a contributing cause of depression and one of its most important consequences. Unfortunately, when it comes to solving the problem of feeling isolated, people are often caught in a vicious cycle: the lonelier and more desperate for company they feel, the more ill at ease they become at making overtures.

Amanda, twenty-four, sought psychotherapy because she felt depressed and stuck in her life. As she initially described her chief complaint to her psychiatrist, she talked about being depressed and having low self-esteem. She did not mention "loneliness" and indeed the subject did not come up until the third meeting. Let's take a look at her story.

* * *

Amanda lives by herself in an apartment in Boston, having grown up on Shelter Island, New York, with her parents and sister. Although she is well-dressed, articulate, and attractive, she looks depressed and thinks of herself as overweight. She graduated from college two years ago and works as a low-level secretary in a small environmental law firm.

After flourishing academically and faring well socially at a small New England college, Amanda decided that she needed to master the art of living on her own before she could expect to live with a boyfriend or roommate. This conviction was fueled in part by the fact that she had some trouble getting along with her college roommates. Also, her parents had implied she was a bit "touchy," and would have to develop more tolerance if she wanted to get along in the world.

When she began therapy, Amanda could barely stop crying because, she said, she felt like such a failure. She hated her job and found living in Boston unnerving because she wasn't sure how to go about making friends. Her law firm was so small, and all eight people who worked there were so much older, that she believed no one could understand her social needs, and she rarely talked from the heart about her loneliness. Going to films, lectures, or dances on her own made her feel like a social reject, so she tended to spend most evenings and weekends alone in her apartment hoping no one would detect how empty her life had become.

Frequently, Amanda would telephone her old hometown boyfriend whom she had dated during summer vacations when she returned home from college. As she reached the end of her college years, she broke off with him because he had no plans for further education and she felt that the two of them were on very different career tracks. When she was lonely, she would call to tell him she wanted to get back together. He made it clear that he was never going to resume an exclusive relationship with her because she had hurt him too much. Thus, he was willing to sleep with her but he would continue to date and have sexual relationships with other women as well. She felt humiliated, hopeless, and isolated—feelings she often confided to her mother during their telephone conversations.

Amanda came to therapy to explore the reasons for her low self-esteem rather than to look into her present barren life situation and how to change it. But a recurring motif quickly emerged in her sessions: "If I never learn to like myself and live alone, how will I ever be able to live with someone else and love them?"

Unfortunately, clinical experience with young people like Amanda indicates that, because of the loneliness it engenders, living alone is often so depleting that socializing becomes increasingly difficult and building relationships grows less likely. Amanda's story eloquently demonstrates the role shame plays in exacerbating loneliness. The more ashamed she feels about being lonely, the more reluctant she is to let anyone close to her for fear they will discover her embarrassing secret.

After admitting to herself and her therapist how lonely she felt, Amanda was able to generate and act upon some possible solutions, like working part-time as a waitress at a restaurant where most of the staff was her age and in a similar phase of life.

The feeling of loneliness is by no means limited to those who live alone. A surprisingly high number of psychiatric patients suffer from isolation and the malaise of not feeling fully known by anyone. Although marriage or living with a companion may protect an individual from the deep loneliness of total isolation, a pervasive loneliness can exist despite the presence of a spouse or roommate. This type of loneliness is rooted in the absence of a wider circle of confidantes with whom one feels well known and accepted. The danger of depending on one individual to keep loneliness at bay is that the relationship can become tense and overstressed, laced with feelings of resentment and claustrophobia.

A second type of loneliness develops in a marriage if one spouse decides that his problems are too burdensome to impose on the relationship. He may then take his troubles to a therapist only to find that by concealing his distress from his mate, he drains the marital relationship of its vitality and purpose. Joseph's story illustrates how this can happen.

*  *  *

A forty-five-year-old executive, Joseph lives in a well-to-do suburb close to Philadelphia. He is quiet, self-contained, and dresses impeccably. Joseph is married to a nurse involved in many community activities. He is the father of two children, both of whom are doing well. In fact, the older child is preparing to go to college at the time Joseph decides to consult a psychiatrist.

In his initial consultation, he complains that he is sinking into a depression and says that he can't risk telling anyone about it. He adds that his wife has too much to worry about as it is, carrying the main responsibility for the two children and her full-time job. Later, he confides that his wife has been so involved in dealing with her own mother's depression that she has little patience left for him.

Joseph is convinced that he has a serious psychiatric illness and thinks that he needs medical treatment to tolerate his depression. It is our impression is that he has a legitimate reason to be sad and that he would benefit from talking about his feelings with his wife.

When he is asked what he thinks might be the source of his sadness, Joseph mentions his anxiety about his daughter's impending departure for a college in California. He says that while he didn't want to squelch her choice, her decision to attend a school that is six hours away by plane has left him feeling sad beyond belief. His job does not allow much time off and he is sure he won't see her very often. If she had chosen a school closer to home, this wouldn't have been a problem.

As he describes how much he will miss his daughter, his eyes fill up with tears. When asked the obvious question—"Don't you think your wife is feeling the same way and that you should tell her how you feel?"—he says he doesn't think she feels the same way, and that he is sure she would perceive his feelings as a burden. He acknowledges that he sometimes feels angry that he is last on her list, but he understands that she has her hands full with the children, her relatives, the neighbors, and her patients. He feels ashamed of being so needy, and requests antidepressant medication.

Joseph is convinced that disclosing the sorrow he is experiencing around one of the major milestones in his married life—namely, the departure of the oldest child—would put too much strain on his closest relationship (although the closeness might be debated). His loneliness is exacerbated because he has fallen out of touch with his own parents, even though they live nearby. He feels they have ignored his children over the years. In his words, they "can't be bothered." In a joint therapy session, Joseph's wife reveals that she feels it is her husband who has actually neglected his parents and that they have retreated from him and his family because of their hurt feelings. His wife is not sure that the relationship with his parents can ever be repaired.

Joseph's story illustrates the increasing difficulty of mending relationships once the rhythm of a routine has been breached. Like Joseph and his parents, each party accumulates hurt feelings and, over time, such feelings can become paranoid. What starts off as "Why don't my parents want to see me and my family more often?" is eventually transformed into "They're self-centered and oblivious and I wouldn't want my children to be exposed to such selfish people." We will continue Joseph's story in a subsequent chapter about how loneliness develops in a marriage.

In later chapters we will also talk about ways of building routines into everyday life that give relationships a chance to deepen, instead of dying from lack of contact. Based on experiences in our own lives and our work with patients, we believe that a pattern of shared tasks provides the opportunity to build up the kind of closeness that happens only when people matter in each other's daily lives, whether in the workplace, at home, or in the neighborhood. We have fooled ourselves into thinking relationships can thrive if they are free of obligation or mutual tasks. In fact, in today's world of too much work, people do not really have time to pursue relationships without some mutual purpose. We will explore ways of creating common ground to infuse energy into existing relationships and to build new ones. We want to show that it is possible to keep relationships vital and exciting even when time is at a premium.

As we describe the ways in which mutual projects and tasks keep people involved with each other, a question arises: Does this position mean we can never expect a relationship to work unless we are doing things for each other? In fact, does it mean we have to buy a friendship with good deeds?

When these objections are raised to our notions about creating common ground, we usually reply: "If you want to enjoy strong relationships you have to matter enough in other people's daily lives so you're not just an extra indulgence that they could perfectly well do without."

Devoid of a predictable context in which to flourish, relationships start to feel as if they are floating in space, without any orienting events to anchor them. This is why long-distance relationships gradually assume a sense of surrealism unless the individuals involved manage to see each other regularly and do things together. We will discuss the kinds of mutual projects that provide a backdrop against which intimacy can unfold.

We will also discuss some of the consequences that have emerged in our society from so many people experiencing feelings of loneliness. As previously mentioned, we see an increase in the number of people seeking psychotherapy or medicine to ease their depression without necessarily appreciating the causal role that isolation may play. The relationship established with the therapist may well relieve the immediate loneliness, but unless the patient's lack of social connectedness is addressed and unless a ripple effect is created in which the therapeutic relationship leads to real reciprocal relationships in the patient's life, there will be no "cure." Because we know that people need to be supported within a web of multiple relationships to successfully meet different needs at different times, no single relationship can be counted on to fully relieve the pain of deep loneliness.

A second consequence of social isolation is that we thirst for exposure to the intimate details of other people's lives and, as a corollary, we develop a compulsion to share such details of our own lives with total strangers. Whether we look at the topics discussed on the *Oprah Winfrey Show* or notice the public invitations to attend meetings issued by Survivors of Incest support groups in local newspapers, we are bowled over by the seeming disappearance of the practice of revealing certain kinds of private material ("dirty laundry") only to family or very close friends.

When people lack a variety of relationships characterized by differing degrees of closeness (each accompanied by its own "grapevine" of gossip), they become starved for the intimacies of private lives; to satisfy their hunger, they turn to television or other media. Research studies conducted at the University of North Carolina in 1988 indicate that shy and lonely people use television viewing as a kind of social compensation for the absence of companionship.[7] While this habit helps them pass time and escape from their worries, in the long run it decreases their self-respect. Perhaps the reason so many people despise themselves for watching too much television is that they recognize it as a pathetic substitute for real friendship.

A third consequence of the epidemic of loneliness, one that particularly affects people in their twenties and thirties, is the difficulty many individuals encounter today in finding a partner for marriage or an intimate relationship. A glut of dating services and personal ads have developed as a substitute for the once elaborate social mechanisms used to introduce eligible young men and women to each other. Men and women of all ages need these traditional mechanisms, yet it appears that there is no longer enough of a social fabric (woven from the strands of religion, family, and friends) to provide this service. Meanwhile, stories abound of people meeting dangerous strangers through ads, dating services, or singles' bars.

Most parents dislike the idea of their adult son or daughter meeting a potential partner through such crude channels, but there is often little alternative. Further, the discouragement and depression engendered by such a search makes it harder to "sell oneself" on the dating market. Once people have been scarred by loneliness, they often fear intimacy, since it always carries with it the potential for another loss and the recurrence of loneliness.

Why has the number of Americans who live alone or feel alone increased so dramatically? Although some might argue that living alone does not necessarily correlate with increased loneliness, most studies indicate that people living alone are significantly more lonely.[8] It does seem clear that whether we are referring to lonely people who live by themselves or lonely people who live with others, there is a silent, growing sector of our population which must contend with loneliness as a constant feature of daily life. Sadly, those who fall into this group often feel too ashamed about their predicament to actively seek relief. We will discuss different kinds of solutions that can prove helpful for people in a variety of situations that typically induce loneliness.

Finally, we will expand on the observations of the Harvard professor mentioned earlier, Robert Putnam, and other researchers who imply that when people turn away from community civic organizations and concentrate only on themselves or their nuclear family, the structures of democratic government are devitalized because there is not enough energy flowing from the voters. We will discuss the way in which mutual tasks in the community are essential for continuing our uniquely American way of life. From our point of view, the danger of our "therapeutically oriented" society is that individuals and nuclear families focus so thoroughly on self-improvement that they forget the necessary maintenance functions involved in taking care of a community so it works well. When people do things for "the common good," making social connections that can deepen into enduring relationships happens naturally.

# 2 The Roots of Our Fear of Dependency

In America today, the adjective *dependent* is suspect. We have transformed a term commonly defined as "needing or relying on someone for support or aid" into an umbrella concept embracing psychopathology, developmental failure, and moral weakness. Our society frequently associates the term with substance abusers, the permanently disabled, and those who simply cannot manage in today's world. Indeed, many people who seek psychotherapy worry that they are too dependent in their lives and they fear psychotherapy will become a crutch as well.

Our national abhorrence of dependency is a relatively new phenomenon. While independence and self-sufficiency are revered values that hark back to the founding of America, they have always stood side by side with the notions of community and helping one another. That balance no longer exists. We believe that this fundamental negative shift in the public's perception of the notion of dependency lies at the root of our national epidemic of loneliness.

In his book, *The Pursuit of Loneliness,* published in 1970, Philip Slater described a society at the "breaking point." He asserted that "three human desires...are deeply and uniquely frustrated by American culture; namely, the desire for community, the desire for engagement, and the desire for interdependence." Slater wrote that this sad state was the direct result of a society reaching for a competitive extreme, a society in which the denial of human interdependence is thoroughly embedded in everyday life and thought. In his words,

> We seek a private house, a private means of transportation, a private garden, a private laundry, self-service stores and do-it-

13

yourself skills of every kind. An enormous technology seems to have set itself the task of making it unnecessary for one human being ever to ask anything of another in the course of going about his daily business. Even within the family, Americans are unique in their feeling that each member should have a separate room, and even a separate telephone, television, and car when economically possible. We seek more and more privacy and feel more and more alienated and lonely when we get it. What accidental contacts we do have, furthermore, seem more intrusive, not only because they are unsought, but because they are unconnnected with any familiar patterns of interdependence.[1]

The first step in lessening the spread of loneliness lies in understanding how we got where we are today. How have we, as a society, come to regard the notion of dependency with such fear and distaste? What are the historical antecedents of our dilemma? What lessons can we learn from the past and how can we apply them in our efforts to refashion the present?

As early as 1616, Captain John Smith described New England as a place where "every man may be master and owner of his owne labor and land."[2] He envisioned the New World as a place where Englishmen and their families could escape the oppression of working for others in a time of dwindling wages and fewer jobs. In America, families would be able to own their own plots, which they could transform into fertile fields with their own labor. The abundance of available land enabled this vision to become a reality.

In the New World the majority of the land could be held by freeholders (farmer-owners), in contrast to England, where tenant farms owned by absentee landlords were the norm. Gradually, the possibility of working hard and becoming your own master, beholden to no one, took hold. By the eighteenth century it had found its place as a fundamental American value. Perhaps Smith's vision played a part in the eventual glorification of a notion of independence that celebrates a man's ability to run his own enterprise instead of having to depend on someone else for a livelihood.[3]

But though dependency had a negative connotation, mutual interdependence remained an essential ingredient in the struggle for survival that characterized the pre-Revolutionary period. In a time when life was so precarious that parents frequently died by the time their children reached their mid-teens, kinship circles were expanded by creating godparents and other forms of "false kin," who would care for the orphaned children until maturity.

If there was some question about the honesty or competence of the stepparents, they were subjected to "Orphan's Court." On these special court days, the guardians were compelled to submit their accounts for auditing. Court officials acted promptly to protect the estates of orphans when malfeasance was called to their attention. Thus, in the Chesapeake (Jamestown, Virginia) area, a safety net was created to deal with recognized needs.[4]

In New England, interestingly, where life span was longer and families were larger, similar needs were more often fulfilled by real kin, namely the family. Many historians feel the experience in the Chesapeake area, where "false kin" bonds were common, fore-shadowed the later frontier experience in which neighbors took care of each other. MIT historian Pauline Maier claims, "Nowadays, our needs being less overt, (they) are easier to deny and so we neglect human needs that earlier Americans readily acknowledged."[5]

As our history unfolded into the nineteenth century, there were numerous examples of America's capacity to prize independence while simultaneously recognizing the necessity for a "give and take" between family, neighbors, and friends. In the Old World, men were tied into networks of dependencies determined by where they stood in the vertical social hierarchy. Landowners provided lodgings for their tenants and artisans worked for wealthy patrons.[6] In America, where people started anew on an equal footing, the old hierarchies of dependency were replaced by a new set of horizontal dependencies in which men joined voluntary associations structured with charters and constitutions.[7]

The earliest of these were community associations found in town charters, covenants that settlers made with each other to govern fairly and as equals for the good of the community. These town charters served as models for later civic associations and corporations that pooled human and financial resources for some communal good. (There was no penalty or disapproval involved if private individuals happened to benefit financially as long as the public welfare was also served.)[8]

By the nineteenth century America was replete with associations. As de Tocqueville observed, "Americans of all ages, all conditions and all dispositions constantly form associations." He believed this happened because individually citizens in a democracy (as opposed to an aristocracy) were "independent and feeble"; by learning to help one another they could avoid "powerlessness."[9] But even then de Tocqueville recognized the tension between individualism and community that we believe has led to our contemporary overemphasis on self-sufficiency. As he explained in *Democracy in America,*

> Individualism is a calm considered feeling which disposes each citizen to isolate himself from the mass of his fellows and withdraw into the circle of family and friends; with this little society formed to his taste, he gladly leaves the greater society to look after itself....There are more and more people who though neither rich nor powerful enough to have much hold over others, have gained or kept enough wealth and enough understanding to look after their own needs. Such folk owe no man anything and hardly expect anything from anybody. They form the habit of thinking of themselves in isolation and imagine that their whole destiny is in their hands....[Finally], each man is forever thrown back on himself alone and there is danger that he may be shut up in the solitude of his own heart.[10]

Robert Bellah, from the University of California at Berkeley, and four other sociologists extend de Toqueville's thinking into our current era in their book, *Habits of the Heart*. They argue that in fulfilling de Tocqueville's predictions, we have isolated ourselves into "life-style enclaves," groups of people who share similar leisure and consumption patterns in their private lives. In other words, we tend to live in proximity to those who match our economic and social levels and share our interests.

Such homogeneous entities are a far cry from the small towns that characterized our nation's earlier days. In those towns, each individual played an important group role. Consequently, people found themselves knitted together by tradition and religion into a complex social fabric. The authors explain that within a contemporary life-style enclave, people often find that their activities do not contribute to the greater common good. This lack of connection with the broader social community leads to the malaise that continues to afflict people in our society, even when they have "made it" economically and have formed a nuclear family of their own.

In the course of their research Bellah and his colleagues interviewed a variety of Americans from different walks of life to find out what gave meaning to their lives. One of their subjects, Margaret Oldham, a therapist in her thirties from a large southern city, said that she enjoyed her work and felt it gave her life significance. Her view of human relationships, however, reflects the problems of our current notion of psychological maturity which does not allow much healthy interdependence. As she explained,

> I do think it's important for you to take responsibility for yourself. I mean, nobody else is going to do it. I mean people do take care of each other, people help each other, you know, when somebody's sick, and that's wonderful. In the end, you're really alone...[11]

As the authors point out, "this clear-sighted vision of each individual's ultimate self-reliance turns out to leave very little place for interdependence and to correspond to a fairly grim view of the individual's place in the social world." The passage of ten years appears to have

confirmed the validity of their observation. To begin to turn the tide of
loneliness, we need to explore the factors that fuel it. But first, we
should realize that our growing isolation is contrary to the way people
have lived over the centuries throughout the world.

Historian Heinrich Fichtenau provides a vignette of European life
in the Middle Ages that demonstrates the peculiarity of our time.
Unlike as in many cultures that preceded ours, we Americans assume
that ever increasing privacy is a privilege that comes with wealth and
power. Compare our determination to provide a separate room for each
child with the attitude of the Abbot of St. Gall, in the Alps, who lived in
the tenth century. The equivalent of a lord in the religious world, the
abbot wanted lots of company even when asleep; since he was at the
top of the power hierarchy, he arranged to have it.

> The plan of St. Gall shows a spacious house intended for the
> abbot; yet nine beds are drawn in his bedroom. This was not an
> ascetic decision; it was simply a matter of wanting one's people
> close at hand, even at night. We set not great store on eating in
> a crowded dining room and even less on spending the night in
> a common bedroom. In the tenth century, it was a punishment
> to make a monk dine alone. Family, familia and kin provided
> what remains today of greatest importance to children: human
> proximity and security.[12]

Like the Abbot of St. Gall, the immigrants who flocked to our country
in the late nineteenth and early twentieth centuries often found
themselves sharing their sleeping quarters. Social historians Neil and
Ruth Cowan studied the Americanization of Eastern European Jews.
In their description of the generation of Jews immigrating to this
country at the turn of the century, they observed that this group of
immigrants held many values much dearer to them than privacy. The
Cowans wrote,

> "Hospitality was more important to the immigrants than single-
> bed occupancy. Virtually none of the first generation of children

to grow up on these shores knew what it was to have his or her own bed, let alone his or her own room. And no one, except the reformers of course, thought this was particularly strange."

The circumstances which led the Eastern European Jews to shared sleeping quarters differed however from those that affected the Abbot of St. Gall; their situation was frequently dictated by economy while his was rooted in an articulated desire to be always in the company of others. Nonetheless, many immigrants had great difficulty in pulling away from the family home and establishing their own households, even when they could afford to do so. Brought up in close proximity to their relatives, they valued their closeness more than they valued their own privacy.

This tradition—sharing living space with friends and family in need of a home—often continued even after the visitors established firm financial footing. Yet by the time the second generation reached adulthood, approximately 1930 through 1950, those who could afford it started buying their own small houses in the suburbs with separate bedrooms and living quarters, including a different bedroom for each child.[13]

Thus, we see that accepting the goal of greater self-sufficiency and independence has always been an integral part of the process of becoming Americanized, but it has only recently become separated from the notion of interdependence. The goal of not having to depend on others represents one of our most deeply held values, which we start inculcating into our children at an early age. For example, some parents feel embarrassed when even very young children act "too clingy," like the three-year-old who cries and is reluctant to join the group at nursery school.

In general, American children are held and carried less and spend more time in isolation than children of other cultures. Recent developmental psychology research confirms that our culture's independence training leads to many more distressed babies with chronic sleep problems than in cultures where mothers allow children and toddlers to sleep with them for several years.

Boston College researcher Gilda Morelli interviewed a sample of Guatemalan mothers and a sample of U.S. middle-class mothers. She found that security blankets and bedtime rituals do not appear in Guatemalan households (for children between two and twenty-eight months) the way they do in American households.

"When a new baby arrives," she says, "children sleep with another family member or move to a separate bed in the same room, usually with few problems." Commenting on this research, psychologist Edward Z. Tronick notes that "U.S. parents clearly see that kids are stressed when they sleep alone, but the parents seem to accept this as a way to promote a child's independence and self-regulation of anxiety in other contexts."[14]

This value—our emphasis on independence and self-sufficiency—is omnipresent in each childhood developmental stage and is prominent as well in many uniquely American institutions. For example, while most middle-class Americans in the 1950s prided themselves on supporting their children until they reached the age of eighteen, children were also regularly reminded, both directly and indirectly, that they were expected to go out and support themselves after turning eighteen unless they planned to attend college. If the child opted for college, parents often put his or her bedroom to a new use since it was generally understood that the "grown-up " child wouldn't be needing it anymore.

(We must note that children may still need their old rooms in the present economy which makes it hard for grown children to support themselves at eighteen or even much later. Fully one-third of men between twenty and thirty-five now live at home for economic reasons.)

In her seminal book, *The Way We Never Were*,[15] Stephanie Coontz suggests that the closely held notion we Americans have of ourselves as independent and self-sufficient is and always has been a fiction. She compares our ideas with those of other cultures and traces the cultural trajectory of the independence/interdependence conflict in our history. She writes:

The Anglo-American notion that dependence on others is immature, weak, shameful or uniquely feminine is foreign to most cultures. In the world view of these societies independence is antisocial; expressing one's neediness, even codifying it, is the route to social harmony and personal satisfaction for both men and women. The Japanese, for example, have a noun *amae* which means reliance on the goodwill or indulgence of another, and a verb *amaru* which means essentially to ask for such indulgence.

In most precapitalist societies, economic, social, and political interactions were not separable from personal relations. No individual operated independently of the kin group or the local community. Consequently, definitions of self were always contextual, because the self did not pick and choose relations with others; it emerged out of these relations and remained dependent on them. Independence was *feared,* not cherished....

Social customs recognized both the inevitability of dependence and the necessity of dispersing it across society beyond separate couples and even extended family networks. Gift giving was one such custom; it established a relationship that was alternately one-sided and therefore more permanent than an "even" relationship in which accounts are always settled so that any party can leave at any time.[16]

Coontz goes on to describe the American tendency to "even things out." For example, if someone gives us a holiday present of some value, we rush out to the store so we can return a gift of equal value and not be left hanging in a state of indebtedness for any substantial length of time. She reminds us that in certain other cultures (like the San people of the Kalahari desert), it would be a profound insult to *immediately* give a gift in return because it shows an unwillingness to be indebted to others, to bear "the burden of obligation that makes a relationship last."[17]

Taken together, these sociologists and historians picture an America that emphasizes independence from earliest childhood on, combined with a competitive striving for privacy and self-sufficiency (seen as symbols of success), all of which leads inexorably to the pervasive loneliness that afflicts us.

Failure in competition often results in shame and accompanying isolation, but so too does success. In fact, the most successful members of the community are precisely those who have attained the isolating privacy that we value so much. They carry their own burden of shame as well, for their loneliness, if revealed, would identify them as dependent losers.

We have persuaded ourselves that the individual or nuclear family who doesn't "need" anyone is strong, while the person or family who depends on others is weak. But ironically, our notion of ourselves as self-reliant may be mainly a myth of our own making.

In *The Way We Never Were* Stephanie Coontz effectively argues that we Americans have fooled ourselves into thinking that the family or individual could ever really operate apart from a greater social structure. Just as the historians cited earlier emphasize the interdependency characteristic of the 1700s, Coontz also describes the way in which patterns of borrowing, lending, and being obligated to others were woven into the fabric of everyday colonial life. Interestingly enough, in that time as well as ours, a person was marked as successful if favors were owed him or her. However, people in colonial America did not go to the amazing lengths to which we go today to avoid asking favors of others.

Coontz notes that during the 1800s America made the transition to a wage-earning society (the transition Captain John Smith wanted to avoid so that men wouldn't have to be beholden to anyone), and that "patterns of personal dependence and local community assistance gave way to more formal procedures for organizing work and taking care of those who were unable to work, either temporarily or permanently. But the rise of a more generalized market economy did not lessen dependency, nor did it make the family more able to take care of its own in *any* sector of society."

She reminds us that historians call the first half of the nineteenth century the age of association. In that era, both the upper and middle classes created large numbers of extrafamilial mutual aid associations to create a safety net for those in need living away from their extended family. Meanwhile, in the lower class, mutual interdependence was an essential part of everyday life since "black immigrant and native-born white workers could not survive without sharing and assistance beyond family networks."[18]

John M. Farragher, a historian who wrote about frontier life in a small town in Illinois, supports a similar point of view. He notes that so-called "self-sufficiency" was not a family characteristic but a "community experience" because neighbors shared work; "cabin raisings, log rollings, hayings, huskings, harvesting or threshing were all traditionally communal affairs."

As one settler explained it to another, "Your wheelbarrows, your shovels, your utensils of all sorts belong not to yourself but to the public who do not think it necessary even to ask a loan, but take it for granted."[19]

We should compare this scenario with modern suburban life in the Midwest, where each family has its own garden implements and strives not to borrow anything substantial from its neighbors for fear of being considered "moochers."

Our popular image of the American family who moved to the suburbs in the 1950s and achieved "the American Dream" is equally spurious according to Coontz. In fact, upward middle-class mobility in the 1950s was fueled by an unprecedented program of governmental handouts. The benefits of the GI Bill were available to 40 percent of the male population between twenty and twenty-four. Young men who never expected to continue their education beyond high school were suddenly able to attend college and embark on careers formerly beyond their reach. Later on, they were able to borrow money at low interest rates for a downpayment on a house.

The government actually shaped the movement of the middle class from the cities to suburbia by additionally funding highway programs, new sewer systems, and utilities programs. This kind of support to the suburbs weakened city services, including public transportation, while strengthening private transport and the suburban model of single family homes.

Once again we see the expression of a deep-seated American value that goes like this: if you're upwardly mobile, you should try to have a life which is separate, private, and self-sufficient, with as little sharing as you can possibly manage. Yet in reality this supposed independence rings false. American families remain dependent, but on distant governmental bureaucracies rather than on their friends, relatives, and neighbors.

Finally, the widespread notion exists that these privileges should be the birthright of every man and woman, ensured and encouraged by a government that sees the perceived independence of individuals and nuclear families as one of its highest goals.

But as previously mentioned, historians remind us that "private values and family affections forming the heart of public life is not at all traditional. It represents a sharp break with Enlightenment thought and the early tradition of our republic which held that public values— the transformation of private interests into contractual obligations and political compacts—were qualitatively different from and superior to private values of love and personal nurturance."[20]

As John Adams said, "the foundation of a virtuous republic must be a positive Passion for the public good....Superior to all private Passions."[21]

In the late 1800s (a period some say bears an unhappy resemblance to our own 1970s–1990s), the growth of conspicuous consumption and selfish materialism led to a middle-class retreat from social reform and an overidealization of private life. Stephanie Coontz writes that this triumph of the individual and nuclear family was a "halfway house on the road to modern 'me first' individualism and a step away from a time when people were expected to have a large portion of their energy involved in civic responsibility for each other." She believes that the "cultivation of private family life represented a repudiation of larger social and political obligations and accelerated the social atomization that has produced modern extremes of individualism."[22]

More recently, our idealization of independence and self-sufficiency has received additional support from a growing psychotherapeutic tradition. The psychological exploration of the self with the aim of achieving greater personal satisfaction has had an important influence on American culture over the last eighty years. In her book *Can't We Make Moral Judgments,* philosopher Mary Midgely coins the expression "therapeutic individualism." She sounds a bit bemused by the idea that "special protection [from all external obligations] is held to be necessary while the self is under reconstruction"[23] and by the notion that a person must learn to accept him or herself before trying to love someone else.

These common assumptions, when layered upon our historical yearning for self-reliance, lead to a curious phenomenon. Upon confronting an obstacle in their passage through life, many Americans try not to impose on their loved ones, friends, or close relatives. They purposefully avoid seeking assistance or solace from the very groups that have traditionally served as the richest source of support and guidance. Instead, they pay a counselor, therapist, psychiatrist, or other professional to give them "expert" advice.

There is no doubt that many conditions require or benefit from professional attention. What is debatable is whether we ought to devitalize some of our most intimate relationships by saving our important confidences for a professional rather than our closest friends and relatives.

In *Habits of the Heart,* the authors point out that weaving together the traditions of self-reliance and psychotherapy leads to the novel phenomenon of treating the old social normative expectations, such as relying on family and friends for support, as "so many [random] alternative strategies of self-fulfillment. What has dropped out are the old normative expectations of what makes life worth living."

In other words, people don't hold themselves accountable to any moral expectations about what makes a successful citizen or a good family member or an excellent worker. Instead, they search for what they think will make them happy. If this means leaving one's community for a "life-style enclave" where a heavy emphasis on creature comforts and a paucity of community connections are the norm, so be it. Each decision becomes a matter of personal preference. As Robert

Bellah and his coauthors observe, "Even relations between parents and children are matters of individual negotiation once the children have left home."[24]

In contemplating alterations in the parent-child relationship at the point when the child becomes an adult, it is interesting to note the strong message of isolation and individualism delivered in the writings of Ayn Rand, an author who is frequently cited by college students as an important influence on their lives:

> There is nothing to take a man's freedom away from him, save other men. To be free, a man must be free of his brothers. That is freedom. That and nothing else. (*The Anthem*).

> The first right on earth is the right of the ego. Man's first duty is to himself....The only good which men can do to one another and the only statement of their proper relationship is—Hands off! (*The Fountainhead*)[25]

Rand's continuing popularity with America's youth leads us to surmise that by the time they reach college, these young people have already accepted the equation: success equals isolated self-sufficiency.

Our cultural tradition bears countless other pieces of evidence illustrating the high value we place on independence and individualism. Anne Swidler, a sociologist at Stanford University, observes that from the cowboy to the hard-boiled detective, our mythical heroes are usually loners who must stand outside of society's bounds to keep their objectivity and to sniff out criminals and bring them to justice. Clearly, these heroes do not pursue selfish individualism but instead, a noble selflessness. As Swidler points out though, "It is part of the profound ambiguity of the mythology of American individualism that its moral heroism is always just a step away from despair";[26] furthermore, that despair is firmly grounded in the hero's mistrust of the community around him.

To conclude our exploration of the roots of our national distaste for dependency, we need to remind ourselves that the first members of each family to emigrate to America *had* to be "tie breakers." In choosing to embrace the adventure of starting fresh in a brand new place, they had to be willing to give up the comfort of being known, recognized, and tied into a larger family unit and its surrounding community. The first step of "coming to America" involved practicing individualism in the extreme. As each relative arrived to join an enlarging family group, individualism and courageous independence became less of a requirement. Yet the glorification of those qualities remained an important part of the process of willingly breaking ties, a process recapitulated over and over again throughout our history as Americans moved the frontier farther west. Essentially, the whole country would never have been settled if Americans hadn't idealized concepts like "going your own way" and "forging your own path."

To understand why "rugged individualism" continued to flourish as a popular philosophy even after the land had been settled and complete families felt rooted here, we need to look at the myth of the American melting pot and to acknowledge that we have never actually blended into a homogeneous people. In countries where heritage, perspective, and skin color are more likely to be shared, there is less need to build a code of tolerant avoidance into the culture. A population whose common background includes a huge body of shared assumptions is much less in danger of inadvertently offending or provoking one another.

In our country, with a population composed of people with hundreds of different ethnic backgrounds, we ought to be both astonished and proud that we can live elbow-to-elbow and avoid the chronic state of war we see today in Bosnia or certain parts of the Middle East and Africa. Some might argue that America's outbreaks of violent crime represent our own version of a chronic state of war, but the casualties of crime do not amount to a war by any stretch of the imagination.

Instead, we have built up a set of rules for public etiquette which allows us to live together in relative peace. These rules boil down to a simple idea: "You live your life and I'll live mine but we won't snoop in each other's business. Meanwhile, when we meet in the street we'll nod and smile in a cordial way to transmit our continued state of truce and peaceful coexistence."

In contrast, on a family trip abroad, our children remarked that France was much less friendly than America. They noticed that when they smiled at French grown-ups, the adults frequently failed to smile back as they expected. There were in fact far fewer exchanges of smiles between strangers in France than in America. These observations awakened us to how much effort we Americans invest in signaling our lack of hostile intent to each other. In our heterogeneous culture, a hostile or even curious stare (such as those regularly exchanged at French cafés) could easily be misunderstood as a sign of aggression by someone from a different background, so we simply don't risk it as often as the French do.

However, we have become so fiercely individualistic that we now experience the consequences. Twenty-five percent of our population lives alone.[27] We have a higher percentage of one-parent families raising children under age eighteen than any country in Europe (America: 25 percent, Britain: 17 percent, France and Germany: 11 to 13 percent, and Greece, Spain, and Italy: 5 to 6 percent).[28]

Two stories juxtaposed on the front page of the *Boston Globe* illustrate our conundrum. The first is titled "On Boston's Fringe: Lack of network frustrates new Irish immigrants." It details the absence of "the kind of immigrant network that has long been a cornerstone of Irish-American pride, a symbol of generosity and strong community."

The second story is headlined: "Years after neighbors last saw her, Worcester woman found dead in home." The story begins:

> It can never be said that Adele Gaboury's neighbors were less than responsible.
>
> When her front lawn grew hip-high, they had a local boy mow it down. When her pipes froze and burst, they had the water turned off. When the mail spilled out the front door, they called the police. The only thing they didn't do was check to see if she was alive.
>
> She wasn't.
>
> On Monday, police climbed her crumbling brick stoop, broke in the side door of her little blue house and found what

they believe to be the seventy-three-year-old woman's skeletal remains sunk in a five-foot high pile of trash where they had apparently lain, perhaps for as long as four years.

"It's not really a very friendly neighborhood," said Eileen Dugan, seventy, once a close friend of Gaboury's, whose house sits less than twenty feet from the dead woman's home. "I'm as much to blame as anyone. She was alone and needed someone to talk to, but I was working two jobs and I was sick of her coming over at all hours. Eventually I stopped answering the door."

...When word went around four years ago that Gaboury had moved into a nursing home, there was no one around to stand up and say no.

Although this story portrays an extreme example of a woman who probably needed psychiatric treatment, it also makes an important point about the influence of economic hard times on the level of energy available for connecting with others. Like Eileen Dugan, the neighbor quoted above, women often cannot afford to give away time since they now have to earn bread and butter money for the family.

"The way work is organized and rewarded in America exacerbates consumerism and individual alienation by eating away at family time, neighborhood cohesion and public solidarities," remarks Stephanie Coontz.[29] Women especially have changed their attitude toward involvement in voluntary activities that better the community. While in the 1950s women often liked volunteering for community service as a way of enhancing their status, many are now hesitant to do so. They fear that if they donate their time and talents, their efforts will be perceived as a public demonstration of low self-esteem since unpaid work seldom garners much respect in our culture.

It seems that our reverence for independence and individualism may have gone too far. Our country was founded on a deep appreciation for self-sufficiency, yet this appreciation was tempered by necessity; settlement of the new land required a great deal of interdependence in the settlers' daily lives. In the nineteenth century, we experienced the

Civil War and the Industrial Revolution. In each of these events, individual freedom was further glorified as old hierarchies crumbled and gave way to a rising middle class. Eventually, there was a rending of the old social fabric which led in turn to our current situation, a society lacking in the very social and political obligations which used to have an orienting effect on individuals and families.

Steven Brill, the founder of Court TV, has remarked that "the collapse of unions, political clubs and church groups has left people very lonely. Events like the O. J. Simpson case [when televised] provide a substitute for the kind of contact these institutions used to provide."[30]

In other words, people feel so alone that they count on televised spectacles to provide a common bond, no matter how tentative.

Christopher Lasch, in his 1979 book *The Culture of Narcissism*, also argues that we Americans are not as independent as we imagine ourselves to be. He describes, however, a shift in the nature of our dependence, beginning with the New Deal. He shows how we have relied on a series of institutions for support—the workplace, the neighborhood, home and, most recently, a new group of professional experts who supposedly hold the key to how people can live content lives.[31]

Since we as psychiatrists are part of the army of experts that Lasch claims has played a crucial role in obliterating people's faith in their own judgment, let us describe the patterns we have seen in our own practices that motivated us to write this book. People often come to therapy voicing a general complaint of depression which they attribute to feelings of "low self-esteem." Frequently they live isolated and lonely lives but they are loath to admit that this is a problem, even to themselves. They are embarrassed and ashamed of their loneliness. Often their lives have not taken any particularly strange or unusual turns, leaving them with no clue as to how they got into this position.

The goal of self-sufficiency, of not asking favors or imposing on others unless absolutely necessary, is so ingrained that most Americans don't give it a second thought and certainly would never see it as a possible cause for their depression. Yet our national cultivation of self-sufficiency often intensifies the pain of common life transitions in which loneliness cannot be avoided. Examples of such transitions include divorce, widowhood, and a first job after high school or college.

Furthermore, most people don't realize that social isolation is depleting, depressing, and bad for their health. In contrast, it is acceptable these days to consult with a therapist hoping to discover the origins of one's "low self-esteem." Most therapist-patient pairs are able to come up with a multitude of plausible causes if they embark on an exploration of the person's past.

This search for causes of low self-esteem can sometimes miss the boat entirely by neglecting the crucial role that loneliness plays in many episodes of depression. Sometimes the patient is ashamed to admit his feelings of loneliness. Sometimes the therapist assumes that the loneliness is the result rather than the cause of the depression or low self-esteem. At still other times, the therapist may be battling a sense of isolation in his own life which clouds his vision of the role isolation plays in his patient's life.[32] If the therapist considers as unimportant questions about how often a patient initiates social contacts, asks favors, or "schmoozes" with people on a day-to-day basis, the process of laying down a social network with friends and acquaintances remains unexamined and unlearned.

We began to appreciate the crucial role that loneliness plays in many of our patients' lives and to realize that most of them had no idea how they had arrived at a chronic state of isolation. We then felt compelled to bring together new research on the importance of social bonds to our physical and mental well-being with what sociologists already know about the role of individualism in our history and value system. We hoped that if we learned more about the factors leading so many of us into isolated lifestyles and clearly identified the price we pay for living this way, we could then begin to move beyond the feelings of shame that prevent us from confronting our loneliness and take steps to shed lifelong habits of "going it alone."

# 3  The Hazards of Loneliness

As the patterns of community life in America change, the illnesses that we die from change along with them. A powerful body of research focuses on the impact of social isolation on both mortality rates and on the frequency and progression of a variety of diseases. Related studies offer insight into the specific changes that occur in our immune functions when we experience isolation. Such changes may eventually prove to be the underlying bridge through which our social world affects our physical health.

## The Roseto Effect

Roseto, a small Italian-American town in eastern Pennsylvania, was founded in the 1880s by immigrants from Roseto Val Fortore, a southern Italian village perched in the foothills of the Apennines. The Rosetans came to Pennsylvania to work in the slate quarries. Socially excluded by the local English and Welsh communities, they established a town of their own. Their town not only prospered but also developed an exceptional community spirit, partly attributed to the stewardship of Father Pasquale de Nisco, a Catholic priest who nurtured civic as well as religious responsibility. Father de Nisco emphasized the importance of American citizenship, education, and the creation of mutual aid societies.

In contrast to the diversity that evolved in several neighboring communities, Roseto remained ethnically and culturally homogeneous through the early 1960s. Residents continued to nurture close family ties and a strong sense of community. Their social lives remained largely family-centered. Three-generation households were the norm.

Even the wealthy avoided ostentatious display, and nearly everyone purchased their goods and services from local businesses.

The placement of the houses themselves further affirmed the interwoven social fabric of life in Roseto. Along Garibaldi Avenue, the main street of the town, "the houses are close together and near the street, so that residents sitting on their porches can talk readily with neighbors and passersby while they watch the town's activities."[1] Comments made by Rosetans to medical researchers also emphasized their sense of cohesion and mutual support:

> I like the people all sociable and with a good heart, religious, like a big family all raised together.

> Where else can you go where your friends and relatives all help out in time of trouble? Everyone trusts everyone else.[2]

Researchers arrived in Roseto in 1962 following a chance encounter between Dr. Benjamin Falcone, a local physician, and Stewart Wolf and John Bruhn, two faculty members from the University of Oklahoma Health Sciences Center. In a conversation with the two scientists, Dr. Falcone observed that Rosetans rarely experienced heart attacks, a sharp contrast to his patients in neighboring Bangor, Pennsylvania. This observation sparked an extraordinarily detailed study of the social customs and health characteristics of Roseto and two nearby towns, a study that eventually encompassed a period of fifty years: 1935 to 1985.[3,4]

In the initial phase of the study, information recorded in death certificates dated from 1935 to 1965 confirmed Dr. Falcone's impression: The rate of death from heart attacks in Roseto was 40 percent lower than the rate in neighboring communities, including the town of Bangor which shared the same water supply, doctors, and hospital.

The researchers than turned their attention to factors that might explain the difference. They considered the possibility that the Rosetans were protected by some unknown genetic trait, but this thesis did not hold up. Rosetans who had moved away from their community lost their protection against heart disease and close relatives who lived in towns like Bangor never enjoyed it.

The researchers also examined a detailed complex of health-related behaviors. For example, not only were participants questioned about food consumption and cooking practices, but their answers were verified by visits to local food stores and the observation of mealtimes in several families. The data showed no meaningful differences between the residents of Roseto and Bangor in health habits or other known heart-disease risk factors. The differences in mortality seemed to be due to distinctions in culture and social connections. As Bruhn and Wolf wrote in 1979:

> One striking feature did set Roseto apart from its neighbors, however, namely its culture, which reflected tenaciously held Old World values and customs. We found that family relationships were extremely close and mutually supportive. This cohesive quality extended to neighbors and to the community as a whole. There was a well-defined man-woman relationship in Roseto, where the man was uncontested head of the family. The elderly were cherished and respected, and they retained their authority throughout life. The atmosphere of Roseto was gay and friendly and reflected an enthusiastic and optimistic attitude toward life.[5]

Despite these strengths, Roseto was not everyone's idea of paradise. Those who achieved professional status often moved to less interdependent communities, where displays of success were less constrained. Others distanced themselves from the culture by choosing spouses from different ethnic groups. When asked why her five daughters married non-Italian men, a ninety-two-year old woman responded by describing her own life. In her account she highlighted the extent to which she had been dominated, first by her parents and then by her husband.[6]

When researchers began studying Roseto in the early 1960s, interviews with teenagers and young adults suggested that these young people would soon turn away from their old community traditions to become more like their "typical" American neighbors. In 1963, the researchers made an important prediction: as family and community bonds loosened, Rosetans would lose their relative protection from death by heart attack.

The prediction proved correct. From 1965 to 1974, the expected decrease in social cohesion became apparent as Rosetans turned outward from family and town. Deaths from heart attacks increased dramatically, particularly in young men and elderly women. The effect of a community's social cohesion on heart disease has subsequently become known as the "Roseto Effect."

Once again, Roseto's architecture reflected and furthered its social transformation. Newer houses, larger and more elegant than the earlier ones, were built on the edge of town, separated from one another by expanses of green lawn. One housewife spoke wistfully of the irreversible change:

> I'm sorry we moved. Everything is very modern here, very nice. I have everything I need, except people. When we lived in town, the neighbors were always in my kitchen or I was in theirs. We talked. We knew what was going on, and there was always someone around to help you and to keep you from feeling lonely. I miss that, but I guess I will never go back.[7]

## Social Ties and Good Health

An expanding body of research confirms that our connections to those around us have many important effects on our health. In the mid-1970s, researchers began to bring together evidence for these effects from a wide range of previously disconnected studies. Dr. Sidney Cobb of Brown University concluded his 1976 presidential address to the American Psychosomatic Society with the following exhortation:

> "There appears to be enough evidence on the importance of social support to warrant action....[W]e should start now to teach all our patients, both well and sick, how to give and receive social support."[8]

Cobb's paper was one of two published that year that gathered together for the first time a remarkably diverse set of studies. These studies seemed to provide compelling evidence that wide-ranging health benefits can accrue from a broad spectrum of social involvements (for example, marriage, contact with relatives, friendship), all of which are grouped together under the researcher's term *social support*.

The title of one of the papers is revealing: "The Contribution of the Social Environment to Host Resistance."[9] The author, Dr. John Cassel, an epidemiologist at the University of North Carolina, pointedly used the language of immunology to frame his argument. The field of immunology, the study of the body's own defenses against disease, was exploding with new insight and information in the 1970s. This expanding knowledge led many health researchers to embrace an important shift in perspective. After devoting decades to a direct assault on the agents of disease (with many impressive results), researchers expressed a renewed interest in defining the natural factors that might act to sustain health.

This heightened interest in the science of immunology offered social science researchers a powerful new metaphor to describe the protective effect that social networks seemed to have on health. The possibility began to emerge that the immune system itself might be the link between our social experiences and our physical health. This renewed interest resulted in an outpouring of new research focused on the relationship between social support and health. Social support was even declared "a contender for the theme of the 1980s"[10] in a 1986 book titled *The Healing Web*.

Summarizing the lessons learned from this new research is no easy task. As social scientists scrutinize the notion of social support and the impact it has on our physical well-being, phenomena that once seemed simple now look considerably more complex.

There are two major complications implicit in social support research. We can quickly illustrate the first by examining the relationship between social isolation and depression. The idea that our social circumstances affect how we feel is certainly not a new one. Modern sociology began with Emile Durkheim's 1897 study connecting the suicide rate to a state of being that he called "anomie," essentially a breakdown of social connection.[11] The notion that social connections are important to good mental health has a certain common sense appeal, and many subsequent studies have confirmed this correlation.

The problem is that it is difficult to move from correlation to cause. If we prove only that two phenomena correlate, we learn nothing about causes. Social isolation could certainly cause depression, but depression might instead be the cause of social isolation. For that matter, they both could be caused by some yet undiscovered factor in a person's genes or experience and have no direct effect on each other at all.

The second complication is an ongoing debate about how to define and measure social support. What aspects of our social world really matter when it comes to our health? Is it the objective measure of how many people we actually see each week? Is it the subjective feeling that there are people we can count on? Are we better off with many friends or with just a few with whom we feel really close? What is "closeness" anyway, and even if we think we know, how do we measure it? Finally, is it possible that all these different aspects of social support might affect different aspects of our health?

With these cautions in mind, we turn to some of the relevant research, beginning with studies centering on physical health and survival. The findings are indeed impressive.

Doctors Cobb and Cassell set the stage for the new wave of research with the publication of their papers in 1976. Each gathered together an array of studies that seemed to show a connection between lack of social support and the occurrence of illness. None of the studies were very impressive on their own. All of them would be dismissed today as showing only correlations, not cause-and-effect.

Taken together, however, they sounded a loud alarm. As Dr. Cobb put it, they offered "hard evidence that adequate social support can protect people in crisis from a wide variety of pathological states: from low birth weight to death, from arthritis through tuberculosis to depression, alcoholism, and other psychiatric illness. Furthermore, social support can reduce the amount of medication required and accelerate recovery and facilitate compliance with prescribed medical regimens...."

Acknowledging that one or two of the studies presented might turn out on further investigation to be truly irrelevant, he concluded that "the series is so long and so diverse that it demands attention."[12] In fact, while more than "one or two" of the studies might be considered irrelevant today because of design flaws, the series did get the attention it deserved. That attention spawned a new generation of studies that go a long way toward confirming that social connections are an important factor in our physical well-being.

The evidence comes mainly from two types of research: longitudinal studies surveying the health and social lives of entire communities over many years, and experiments performed on both animals and humans revealing the direct physiological effects of social contact.

Through their community studies, social network researchers have conferred a degree of fame on several other localities in addition to Roseto: Alameda County, California; Tecumseh, Michigan; Evans County, Georgia; Gothenberg, Sweden. Each has been the site of a long-term "prospective" study looking at the relationship between social involvement and mortality over periods of time ranging from ten to thirteen years. The length of time that these communities were studied, combined with the variety of measures used to assess the subjects' health at the inception of the studies, helped to distinguish isolation that was the result of medical illness from isolation that contributes to the development of a future illness.

From the collective evidence of these ambitious studies, a simple and powerful fact emerged: Isolated individuals are likely to die sooner than their more socially involved neighbors. This stark conclusion could not be explained away by any differences in health between the two groups at the beginning of the studies or by the influence of "unhealthy lifestyles" (smoking, lack of exercise, alcohol use, obesity, or poor diet) on those who were more isolated. The early deaths of isolated people appear to be a direct result of isolation itself.

In 1988, a summary article appeared in the prestigious journal

*Science*. In it James House, chair of sociology at the University of Michigan, and two colleagues reviewed the subject of "Social Relationship and Health." They found that there is "a remarkable consistency of the overall finding that social relationships do predict mortality for men and women in a wide range of populations, even after adjustment for biomedical risk factors for mortality."[13]

This increase in mortality was found in all categories of illness but, as the Roseto project illustrates, special attention has been given to heart disease. In his book *The Broken Heart*, written in 1977, Dr. James Lynch from the University of Maryland Hospital makes the powerful argument that loneliness is a cause of heart disease and that "reflected in our hearts there is a biological basis for our need to form loving human relationships."[14]

Recent research lends further support to Dr. Lynch's claim. Patients who live alone after their first heart attack are almost twice as likely to have a second heart attack or to die from heart disease as those who share a home.[15] Similarly, only half of all patients with heart disease who were unmarried and had no one in whom they confided remained alive after five years, while more than 80 percent of those who were married or had a confidant survived. Again, these results could not be explained by any known medical predictors of heart disease or survival other than social support.[16]

The ways in which social networks affect heart disease can also be illustrated by looking directly at the blood vessels themselves. In a study of both men and women undergoing coronary angiography (an X-ray technique for examining the blood vessels that supply the heart), those patients who reported leaning on family or friends for assistance and those who described a sense of being loved had significantly less atherosclerosis, the fatty deposits along the walls of arteries that can obstruct blood flow and lead to heart attacks.[17] Furthermore, healthy elderly individuals who have a trusting, confiding relationship with at least one other person also tend to have lower cholesterol levels than those without this kind of loving support.

Moving from heart disease to cancer, Dr. David Spiegel, a professor of psychiatry at Stanford School of Medicine, made headlines several years ago when he discovered that women with metastatic breast cancer who attended a weekly support group lived twice as long as those who received routine cancer care (on average, 36.6 months compared to 18.9 months).[19] More recently, UCLA psychiatrist I.F. Fawzy and his colleagues reported similar effects from a series of weekly support groups for patients with malignant melanoma, a potentially lethal skin cancer. In addition, Dr. Fawzy's group found that patients in the support groups had evidence of improved immune function, specifically greater activity of "natural killer cells," a type of white blood cell that helps fight certain cancers.[20] We must therefore turn our attention more directly to the effects of social contact on the immune system.

## Social Ties and Our Immune System

In 1977, a group of researchers in Australia published the first evidence of decreased immune function in "healthy people under great psychological stress."[21] The great psychological stress was the loss of a spouse. The decrease in immune function was a lowered responsiveness of lymphocytes, a type of white blood cell that plays a central role in protecting the body against viruses, tumor cells, and other intruders. This discovery fit well with the fact that serious illness and death increase significantly after the loss of a husband or wife.

Human immune systems are not alone in their vulnerability when stressed by the disruption of social bonds. Several varieties of monkeys show similar changes in immune response when mothers and infants are taken from each other[22] and when "peers" are separated.[23] In the absence of an animal peer, even a kindly laboratory assistant will do. Contact with humans also reduces heart disease in dogs, cats, horses, and rabbits[24]

The Australian group chose to study bereavement not because they were particularly interested in social ties, but simply as a convenient example of a stressful experience. There is, however, good reason to believe that the effects of bereavement on immune function reflect a uniquely important quality of the special importance of close ties.

Fifteen men married to women with advanced breast cancer were followed during their wives' illnesses and for a year after their spouses' death. Even though these men had lived with the severe stress of their spouses' terminal illnesses for many months, measures of their lymphocyte response dropped sharply after their wives died.[25] The actual loss of their spouses brought about a change in immune function that had not occurred over the long months of medical problems and painful anticipation.

The length of time that our immune systems remain impaired is longer following bereavement than after other stresses. Typically, stress produces a drop in immune response that lasts just a few days, even when the stress itself continues. The change in these widowers persisted for at least two months, and other studies have shown an increased mortality for widowers that lasts through the first six months following the death of a spouse.[26]

An internist we know told us about a patient named Anne, who developed metastatic breast cancer in her early fifties. Fortunately, she responded well to chemotherapy and showed no signs of recurrence for over ten years. Then Anne and her husband decided they wanted to live closer to the ocean. They moved away from the community where they had spent most of their lives and settled into a new condominium overlooking the sea. Anne never felt at home in the new location. She found her neighbors unfriendly and the condominium management uncooperative.

When her husband died, she felt alone in her new world. Within months of his death, Anne developed diabetes and began to experience severe bone pains that suggested the return of her cancer. Her weight dropped precipitously, and soon she was dead. (As we examine the effects of the loss of a spouse, however, it is important to note that marriage retains its overall health benefits despite the transient increase in risk when it ends.)

Immune function is affected not only when a husband or wife is lost through death, but also through divorce. Both women[27] and men[28] show lowered immune responses (along with reports of more frequent illnesses) in the year following a marital separation. Once again, these changes cannot be connected to any differences in "health-related behavior" such as weight loss, sleep habits, caffeine intake, or alcohol and cigarette use that we might expect to change when a marriage is ending.

Lowered immune response occurs even with the more limited estrangement that develops within the structure of an intact but unhappy marriage. In a group of married men and women, those with low scores on a test of "marital quality" had poorer immune responses than those in happier marriages. Lonely medical students also show decreases in their immune function.[29]

Before leaving the field of immunology, there is one final study (1988) that we find particularly intriguing. Fifty healthy college students were asked to write in a journal for four consecutive days. Half of the students were told to write about personally traumatic experiences and the other half were asked to write about trivial topics. After six weeks, those who had confronted painful experiences in their writing not only felt better than those who had filled their journals with "small talk," but they also had made fewer visits to the college health service and had better immune function.[30]

Since journal writing is a solitary affair, it may seem that this study has little to say about our social needs. Many writers have observed however that it is impossible to write without writing *to* somebody, even an imagined somebody. In the minds of these students, there must have been a reader or perhaps a listener. This study strengthens the case for the role that psychotherapists have long tried to fill. Of course, it is also a role that good friends and relatives have assumed for even longer.

## Social Ties and Child Abuse

Lack of social connections affects our mental as well as our physical health. Child abuse, sadly, bridges these two realms, since the feelings and behavior of the parent powerfully affect the physical health of the child.

Recent writings about child abuse emphasize the complexity of the phenomenon and sometimes describe it as an "ecological" problem in which abuser and child interact with a larger family, social, and economic environment.[31, 32] Within this complexity, the importance of social isolation is becoming clear. A group headed by pediatrician Eli Newberger at Children's Hospital in Boston compared children who were hospitalized for child abuse, domestic accidents, failure to thrive, and poisoning (what the researchers call "pediatric social illnesses") with children hospitalized for more straightforward medical problems. Reflecting on their findings, they wrote:

> Although we found evidence that all categories of pediatric social illnesses are characterized by some isolation of case families from their kin and communities, this isolation was most pervasive in the families that bear the diagnosis of abuse.... [Abusive mothers] may have seen their relatives less often, felt that no one was interested in their problems, have suffered a recent death in the family, coped alone with child care, and disagreed with their husbands concerning discipline and child rearing. They could count on few relatives to help and had fewer kin in their communities. More than the mothers in the other case categories, they appeared to see themselves as unconnected to others.
>
> Mothers in a particularly high-risk group labeled the "crisis cluster... were also more likely to feel, at least some of the time, that no one cared what happened to them."[33]

Many other studies confirm a connection between child abuse and social isolation. We must take into account, of course, the problem inherent in the use of correlations that we described earlier. A connection is not proof of cause. Not all of the social isolation experienced by abusive families is imposed on them by an uncaring world; certainly some of it is of their own making. Nevertheless, Dr. Newberger notes that "the more kin one has available, the greater the ecological advantage." The more people around with whom we have some connection to start with, the less likely we are to succeed in driving them *all* away.

Today, with families becoming increasingly mobile and dispersed, we are all less likely to be surrounded by relatives than in the past. And as neighbors share fewer tasks and responsibilities (and are increasingly less likely to mind each other's business), neighborhood connections provide a less reliable substitute than they might have in the past. In recent years, an African saying has become very popular: It takes a village to raise a child. When it comes to preventing child abuse, this sentiment may well be right on the mark.

## Social Ties and Mental Health

Durkheim's early ideas about suicide and social disorganization have held up well for over a hundred years. A remarkable series of studies commissioned by the World Health Organization in the late 1970s examined suicide rates in eighteen countries from 1900 on, a period of dramatic social change. The central conclusion was that social events can affect national rates of suicide by as much as 50 percent, with varying effects on different demographic groups such as the young, the elderly, men, and women. When researchers then looked at fifteen "social variables" that reflect people's sense of connection to each other and their place in a social network (for example, marriage and divorce rates, illegitimate births, unemployment, women's employment, size of different age groups), they discovered that the rate of suicide in a country did indeed rise when family cohesion declined or "anomie" increased. They even developed a mathematical model that "gave surprisingly exact predictions of the increases and decreases of suicide in Europe" over a ten-year period.

Their findings confirmed for whole countries what earlier studies had demonstrated about regions and neighborhoods. People who are less embedded in a social world are more likely to commit suicide. (Some of the individual variables also offer interesting social commentary. For example, it is a statistical fact that suicide rates increase when more people get TVs.)[34]

When we move from suicide to less extreme consequences, findings become a bit murkier. We might expect that social isolation would have a more straightforward impact on our mental health than on our physical well-being, but this is not the case. In fact, the research relating social isolation and mental health is much more confusing, and for a simple reason. Most psychiatric illnesses, from depression to schizophrenia to anxiety disorders, make it harder for people to develop and sustain relationships. Even if we find that persons who develop psychiatric illnesses are socially isolated long before they show evidence of other problems, the question remains: was the isolation a cause of the illness or was it what doctors call a *prodrome*—an early sign of the illness itself?

Individuals with psychiatric problems, particularly depression and the less severe disorders that until recently were called *neurosis*, clearly tend to have smaller social networks and fewer close relationships than most people.[35, 36, 37] Some "prospective" studies have even shown that the lack of social support precedes the development of the illness. An important study of depression in working-class women in Camberwell, England, in the 1970s found that women who had a "confiding relationship" with another adult, whether husband, lover, relative, or friend, were much less likely to become depressed than those who did not have such a relationship. Women with young children at home gained the most from having a confidant, a conclusion that makes immediate sense to many parents.[38]

Furthermore, data from a RAND Corporation project investigating the effects of different health insurance policies on both health and the demand for health services, showed that people who started out with more close friends and relatives used mental health services significantly less over a three- to five-year period than those with fewer "social resources."[39]

The jury is still out, however, on the relationship between depression and social support. A team of researchers recently used a complex mathematical analysis to examine depression in female twins whose births were recorded in the Virginia Twin Registry between 1935 and 1971. They concluded that lack of social supports does not lead to depression. Instead, their model predicts that an underlying unidentified factor (which may be either genetic or environmental) contributes to both depression and poor social networks.[40]

Clearly, we still have much to learn about the nature of depression. While awaiting a better understanding of its underlying causes, we must recognize that depression is ordinarily a treatable condition. One particularly effective treatment approach is Interpersonal Psychotherapy (ITP). A type of brief psychotherapy developed at Yale School of Medicine in the 1970s, ITP is based on the assumption that depression, whatever its fundamental causes, is somehow closely linked to disturbances in an individual's interpersonal world. ITP treatment focuses on restoring or reworking social connections and social roles. Carefully controlled research has shown ITP to be an extremely effective treatment for depression, as effective in the treatment of mild to moderate depression as antidepressant medications.[41, 42, 43]

In other words, if therapists help people who are depressed to look closely at their connections with others and then take action based on what they see (as we will illustrate in a future chapter focusing on psychotherapy), the depression often disappears. Attempts are now under way to extend the use of ITP to several other psychiatric problems. Its effectiveness in these other conditions is still being evaluated, but its usefulness with depression demonstrates that an understanding of the importance of social support has direct and practical value.

### Social Ties: Some Uncertainties and a Simple Conclusion

There is much that we don't yet understand about social support. For instance, we don't know if Dr. Sidney Cobb's original notion that social support protects us from the harmful effects of stress is correct, an idea that is now called the "buffering hypothesis." The other possibility is that social support provides direct health benefits even in the absence of stress. If Cobb was correct, the benefits of social support should be greater for people who are facing particularly hard times in their lives. Unfortunately, some studies support the buffering hypothesis and some findings are better explained by a direct effect. The scholarly debate continues.

Scholars also disagree about what aspects of social support really matter. For example, the RAND study found that "social resources"—the knowledge that close friends and relatives are there for us (sometimes called "perceived support")—is more important than the actual number of social contacts that we have.

By contrast, medical students facing a major exam were protected from increases in anxiety by actual social contacts but not by perceived support.[44] It seems likely that different aspects of social support (which is a complex concept made up of many separate components) affect different facets of our well-being, but no clear picture has yet emerged.

Important parts of the picture are clear, however. Lack of social support leads to increased mortality, increased heart disease, lowered immune function, and increased suicide rates. It is also associated with child abuse and a variety of psychiatric problems.

From this complexity, a simple fact emerges with great power. When we neglect our bonds to family, friends, and neighbors, we take very real risks with our health. Of course, this is an individualist's argument for the importance of community. This belief is based on the value of a strong social network to the individual rather than on its benefits to the larger group.

Still, it is remarkable that the data on social support and health allows such a significant case to be made. Perhaps the convergence of individual and group interests is the natural result of our evolution as social beings, animals who once depended on the group for survival in a dangerous world. It would not be surprising if the importance of the group was reflected in our individual biological natures.

In any case, the emergence of this data over the last twenty years is particularly ironic. As Professor James House and his colleagues observed in their 1988 *Science* article, "just as we discover the importance of social relationships for health, and see an increasing need for them, their prevalence and availability may be declining."[45]

We have demonstrated the medical importance of social ties only to find that our connections to family and to community are precariously weakened by the circumstances of modern life. Or perhaps it is precisely because our social ties are weakening that we begin to notice their importance.

# Part II

# Our Culture's Attempts at Solutions

# 4 Psychotherapy: One of the Possible Cures for Loneliness

"I don't want to be a burden on my children," the newly widowed grandfather sighs.

\* \* \*

The worried mother observes, "My husband already has too much on his shoulders."

\* \* \*

Confused about sexual issues, the teenager won't talk with her mother or sisters because, she says, "They can't handle it right now."

Most of us will find familiar echoes in these poignant remarks. They represent three common situations and are examples of our reluctance to tap our closest relationships for sympathy, solace, counsel, and companionship.

In earlier chapters we explored the origins of an epidemic of loneliness fueled in part by the growing segment of our population that lives alone—currently 25 percent. Here we will explore the ways that psychotherapy has helped to solve the problem of loneliness and the ways in which it has failed.

## Psychotherapy in America

It is no accident that Americans turn to psychotherapy more frequently than do people in any other part of the world. Among other reasons, its popularity is a logical extension of our rigid ideas about not imposing on others. Anxious not to lean on their relatives, the grandfather,

mother, and teenager mentioned above may choose to "get help,"—
that is, to seek the assistance of a mental health professional. For those
who can afford it, psychotherapy is often viewed as a potential cure for
loneliness, on the assumption that it reflects underlying emotional
problems.

There are many theories about why Americans seek therapy more
than people in other countries. Some speculate that we feel more
isolated and disoriented than our counterparts elsewhere because few
of us live out our lives in the place where we were born and where
people knew our family. Our mobility has left us feeling increasingly
isolated and disoriented. Thus, many of us don't have the clear sense of
who we are that comes from being around people who know us well
over a lifetime. Because long-term isolation has a depleting effect, we
are more likely to feel depressed than are people who live in countries
with greater residential stability. Consequently, those individuals who
seek therapy often wish to resolve the question of identity and to relieve
the malaise of not feeling known or understood by oneself.

Eva Hoffman, an editor for the *New York Times*, writes eloquently
about this dilemma in *Lost in Translation,* her memoir about
emigrating to the United States from her native Poland. From her
perspective, most Europeans would not think to question their own
identities since who and what they are is well known to several
generations of friends and acquaintances who have grown up in the
same place. "My American friends," she writes, "watch the vicissitudes
of their identity carefully; now it's firm, now it's dissolving, now it's
going through flux and change." When she is in America, "sometimes
the desire for the comfort of being a recognizable somebody placed on
a recognizable social map breaks in on me with such anguishing force
that it scalds my spirit." A world in which everyone knows everyone
else's history, can be oppressive to those with skeletons in the family
closet which they would rather forget; on the other hand, it certainly
reduces the incidence of "identity crises."[1]

Americans also enjoy a long tradition of being open-minded and
relentless about remaking themselves, a tradition which runs deeper
and stronger here than in other cultures. This is the country that

welcomed most of Freud's followers, making it possible for them to pursue their profession by giving them plenty of business and a nonjudgmental atmosphere in which to practice. Most American immigrants arrived armed with the belief that here they would be able to improve their social and economic situation. As they succeeded, therapy and psychoanalysis offered a way to achieve self-understanding, a promise the newcomers embraced as another road by which they could advance their never-ending pilgrimage toward the ideal life they envisioned.

Unfortunately, by relentlessly continuing our forebearers' penchant for self-improvement, we may have overshot the mark. The prevailing culture that has evolved in America encourages us to present ourselves as self-sufficient. In our eagerness to achieve the desired impression we are often untrue to ourselves, transforming the entire exercise into a charade. In our quest for self-sufficiency we have reached the point where we accept the idea that confiding in a paid stranger, in the guise of a mental health professional, might be superior to imposing our problems on an unpaid intimate.

Inherent in this progression is the danger that our reluctance to share our emotionally "messy" problems with those we know best will in the end increase our feelings of isolation. Fearful to impose on others, we distance ourselves from friends and family. Consequently, we run the risk of sanitizing our friendships and intimate relations to the point where they become artificial. The more we feel that confiding our difficulties will strain the relationship, the greater the effort we invest in restricting our conversation to cheery subjects which do not demand any advice or solace.

Complicating this dilemma is the very real possibility that we have developed an unrealistic level of faith in the mental health profession's capacity to single-handedly resolve life's passionate difficulties. Daily news reports detailing yet another incident of family violence give us reason to doubt that the vast increase in the number of experts has solved most of America's emotional problems. Further complicating the situation is the possibility that many of us enter psychotherapy expecting treatment to dissolve the fears and anxieties we have about forming a social network. We reason that our self-esteem will improve so much through therapy that our new confidence will eliminate the "work" involved in initiating social contacts.

This scenario is an illusion. In reality, the truth is often that the longer one lets social relationships languish, the harder it is to revive them. And it is not uncommon for people in therapy to neglect their "real life" relationships. It is important then to realize that the therapeutic relationship is not a good example of an "ideal" relationship (although it is often idealized by patients), since it carries the hidden and faulty implication that relationships ought not to be reciprocal but that they can be comfortably one-sided.

## The Uses of Psychotherapy

In spite of these caveats, many conditions can indeed benefit from professional intervention. We will not try to review all the conditions that merit therapy. We will focus instead on the relationship between loneliness and depression, and the role therapy can and cannot fill in alleviating the accompanying feeling of despair.

Loneliness, if prolonged, nearly always leads to depression. Many people in our society are actually extremely lonely not because they lack contact with people but because they have no one with whom they can truly "be themselves," no one with whom they can talk about almost anything with little self-consciousness.

Psychologist Sidney Jourard, professor of psychology at the University of Florida in the early 1970s, has argued convincingly that the desire to disclose oneself genuinely to another person is a basic human need and, when that need is stymied, malaise and maladjustment result. Specifically, he said that "to make oneself fully known to at least one other significant human being" is a sign of a healthy personality. He believed that maladjustment is often the active struggle to avoid being known by another.[2]

When a person has friends and acquaintances but no one with whom he is "truly himself," the loneliness that results can wither creativity, exploration, and even the necessary actions required to keep life moving along. At this point, an effective therapist can function as a launching pad, providing the impetus needed to get the patient reconnected in a relationship where he can talk over matters of the heart in the course of his daily life.

The new patient often reports "trouble with relationships." He may not notice the essence of the problem is his own loneliness, which often exists despite the fact that there are apparently plenty of people in his life. It is up to the therapist to detect this problem and then to explain it to the patient. And while it is true that the neurotic patterns leading to loneliness are often rooted in some aspect of the patient's past, a good therapist takes care not to be seduced into searching so thoroughly for traumas in the past that he neglects gathering a complete history in the present.

How then might therapy work to help a person improve his relationships so that eventually one or several of them can accommodate genuine self-disclosure in Jourard's sense of the term? At the outset, we must acknowledge that there is no universal agreement on precisely how therapy works even among therapists or patients. In fact, differences of opinion in the assertions made by various schools of therapy have fueled several current research projects designed to explore this question.

What we do know, however, is that on entering therapy most patients hope to be subjected to some incomprehensible magic, transforming them so that they will never again feel overwhelmed or in despair. If such magic did exist, they wouldn't expect to be able to understand it. This attitude may partially explain the wide allure of a "happiness pill" such as Prozac and the easy acceptance of the idea of correcting a "chemical imbalance," which covers much that is not yet understood about neurochemistry.

Therapists are trained in a variety of disciplines which evolved from some very different schools of thought. When we examine which kind of therapy gets the best results, we discover that there is no single winner. Yet a number of studies do show that the outcome of any type of therapy is likely to be more favorable for a patient who trusts his therapist and feels at ease talking to him. Furthermore, most of us need to feel understood and respected by the therapist if we are to wade through the small, embarrassing details of our worries without feeling despised.

One of the magic parts of therapy then seems to lie in matching the patient with a practioner in whom he feels comfortable confiding. This is not surprising because talking things over is often a necessary prerequisite to stimulating change or adjustment in any area of one's life. As British psychiatrist Anthony Storr has observed, "Putting things into words captures the ephemeral."[3] That is, plans, dreams, and impressions that have wafted by fleetingly can now be scrutinized and harnessed as they are communicated to a fellow human being.

When a person becomes accustomed to the absence of a trusted confidant, he sometimes forgets how essential feedback is in prompting action. For example, children do not progress through many of the usual developmental milestones if there is no one to encourage, praise, and cheer their success. Faced with a new challenge or reviving a skill which has become rusty, even adults need to bounce their thoughts off a sounding board before translating them into action. While children need outright praise and encouragement, most adults identify a lively glimmer in the eye, murmuring sounds signifying attentive listening, and well-placed questions as evidence that they are in the presence of a caring human with whom they can comfortably think aloud.

Over time, as he comes to trust his therapist as a sounding board, the patient finds that he has filled in enough of the details of his personal history so that he and the therapist begin to share a common story of his life. From that story, they begin together to develop theories about what made the people who mattered most to the patient (often parents or siblings) behave as they did. Together they also explore what makes the patient tick. Although the reconstructed story is never wholly accurate, it frequently allows the patient to shed the childhood feeling that events happen without rhyme or reason, that they are determined by grown-ups who don't make any sense. If therapy is able to provide an ongoing structure in which the patient gains understanding of his problems, it may allow him then to replace a childlike feeling of helplessness with adult understanding and effectiveness.

This brings us to the second important way therapy can work. In most human relationships people operate on automatic pilot much of the time, unconscious of the signals they may send. They react to one another and the relationship goes well or badly while each party strives secretly to figure out why the other person responds as he does. Therapy at its best can be like a lab course in relationships. When the patient suspects a particular reaction or feels a particular way, he has a chance to discuss what he is experiencing, to test his perceptions and to figure out how they are influenced by distortions left over from childhood.

The patient plays out this scenario in two arenas. First, he talks with his therapist about his reactions to people in his life outside of therapy. Second, during the sessions he also discusses the way he reacts to the therapist. The most competent practitioners will let patients know when their perceptions of the therapist are correct as well as when they are more likely to be a function of "transference."

(Transference is actually a simple concept. It means that we are not capable of experiencing a relationship as genuinely new and completely free from distortions.[4] Instead, our experience with people in the present is colored by how we experienced important people in the past.)

The more problematic past relationships have been, and the less successful we have been in seeing them clearly, the more likely they are to color our present responses in ways of which we are unaware. For example, a patient who always felt belittled by his mother may accuse the therapist of treating him the same way. Further exploration may then reveal that throughout his life he has distanced himself from women for whom he feels affection because he automatically assumes that if he gets too close they too will belittle him.

An understanding of the use of transference in therapy can help to explain why therapists are so frequently depicted as acting mysterious about their lives, always countering the patient's questions by asking, "Well, what do you think about it?" This secretiveness does not exist just so the therapist can conceal his own quirks. Instead, the therapist refrains from revealing much about himself in order to give the patient a chance to voice his own perceptions so that they can be explored and analyzed before being measured against reality. After the patient's perceptions of the therapist have been analyzed by both parties, it can be helpful for the practitioner to reveal something of himself. If the therapist becomes overly involved in divulging personal information, this lab function of therapy might never be realized.

This discussion does not begin to address the complexity of psychoanalysis, the concepts of cognitive therapy, or the theories behind all the other kinds of therapy available. Instead, it represents an attempt to generalize by focusing on some of the threads common to most therapies. It does not address the question of medication and its effect on depression and isolation, a subject which we will deal with in the next chapter.

It is important to note, however, that the research studies appear to indicate that neither medicine nor psychotherapy alone can be as effective in the treatment of depression as an approach which combines the two. So even though books such as Peter Kramer's *Listening to Prozac*[5] make medicine seem like a savior for those suffering from depression (which in some cases it is), interaction with a therapist appears to bolster the effectiveness of such medications.

Let us return now to a theory broached earlier in this book in order to clarify its relevance to therapy. We believe that when two or more people are involved in a shared task their interaction forms an ongoing context. Furthmore, it is only within such a context that relationships can deepen. Although this seems at first glance a rather simple and obvious idea, its implications are myriad and profound. The sociologist George Homans noticed the same phenomenon when he created a model of social systems which suggested that "activities, interactions and sentiments are mutually dependent on one another and specifically, the higher the interaction between two or more people, the more positive will be their sentiments toward each other."[6] Homans points out that if two people can't stand each other, chances are that one will drop the shared task and the context will subsequently disappear.

These observations are relevant to our discussion of how

psychotherapy works since therapy is a good example of a shared task. Of course, it is an unusual example because both parties do not reveal themselves in the same way. Instead, the patient tells all and the therapist mostly listens, interjecting some well-placed observations or questions. But since both patient and therapist are sharing the task of understanding the patient, therapy provides the context in which the relationship can deepen.

Certainly if therapy is effective, the patient will come to talk more and more freely about himself. The therapist ought not to be too revealing about himself, but he is likely to feel more empathic with the patient as he gets to know him better. This inevitable sense of a deepening relationship is strong stuff and potentially dangerous because the relationship must stay on a professional level to be effective.

Often, the patient starts to feel a bit peculiar. Because it is such a relief and a novelty to talk so freely with an attentive listener, he may start to experience powerful feelings toward his therapist. Even if he doesn't feel "in love" with the therapist, he may start making odious comparisons between the difficult "real" reciprocal relationships in his everyday life (if indeed he has some) and this wonderful relationship in which he doesn't have to worry about the feelings and behavior of a person who has been professionally trained to listen without talking about himself.

Gradually, the patient may come to see the therapy relationship as a blueprint for what a relationship should truly be. He may begin to feel that the real world of "do unto others as you would have them do unto you" relationships is not worth the effort because those relationships demand such hard work. In the extreme, the patient might start to withdraw from his closest real-life relationships, determined to form new ones in which he will be treated more as his therapist treats him. It is a dangerous dynamic, because this type of skewed relationship is not to be found in the "real world."

It is also important that the therapist take care not to be prematurely judgmental or overly directive. One of our patients described to us the cavalier way in which her former therapist encouraged her to act on her negative feelings toward her husband by leaving him, a line of suggestion that nearly destroyed her marriage. Looking back, the patient felt she had been so suggestible to the opinions of her therapist, who seemed quick to categorize her marital relationship as highly flawed, that she was unable to clearly judge whether her marriage was worth saving. She had been so enthralled with the therapist that she temporarily lost track of the positive aspects of her marriage.

But the hazards of psychotherapy mentioned above are just that— hazards. Often a good therapy experience can help a person take stock of his life and encourage him to develop an understanding of how he himself contributes to his life's not progressing as he desires. With the help of a therapist, the patient has the chance to understand the contribution his unconscious distortions make to the course of his life. Equipped with that self-knowledge, he is then free to make more conscious choices about how to go forward.

The more aware the therapist becomes of the potential hazards in psychotherapy, the less likely they are to occur. Most important, the therapist and patient must keep track of the patient's "real relationships" and treat them with proper respect and care so they won't wither away by the time therapy ends, leaving him lonelier than ever.

It may well be that the patient needs to talk about the important insights gained in therapy with the people who matter most in his everyday life, perhaps his spouse or an adult child. The failure to share important material allows these relationships to become devitalized.

If treatment works as it should, a ripple effect may occur in which the satisfaction of talking frankly in therapy leads to a deepening of the patient's relationships in real life. Subsequently, he experiences a greater appreciation for these relationships that now provide a balanced, reciprocal self-disclosure.

## Two Lonely People

To learn more about the role therapy can play in alleviating loneliness, we turn to several of our patients. Let's begin with Jessica, a young woman who came to Dr. Olds complaining of depression and her fear that she would never be able to make a relationship work.

Jessica is an attractive, blond, twenty-nine-year-old psychologist who seemed tentative and skeptical on entering therapy. She said she was often depressed and that she was having a very difficult time deciding whether to break up with her boyfriend because she wasn't sure that she loved him.

A big-framed woman, Jessica expressed worry that her therapist might be too small, tidy, and intellectual for her to feel she could truly "let her hair down." She decided to meet twice a week in spite of her worries once she understood that her fears were based on "transference"; her mother is a meticulous woman who gets overwhelmed in the face of strong (messy) feelings and Jessica unecessarily feared that her therapist would have the same reaction.

Jessica was the middle daughter of three girls. Because her father worked for an international banking company, the family moved frequently when she was young and she lived in a variety of locations in both the United States and Europe. Jessica felt her mother had often been depressed while raising her children, possibly because she felt uprooted from her various homes. She described her mother as a bright woman with very high intellectual standards for all her daughters. The joy in the family seemed chiefly to revolve around music. The mother and all three daughters sang in church choirs.

Gradually Jessica's father started drinking heavily, and he and her mother became progressively estranged. When Jessica was sixteen, her mother sought a divorce.

Jessica had been a very good child and student throughout her formative years. She felt responsible for her mother after the divorce and tried to be her confidant when her mother became depressed. But her attempt to help her mother proved so difficult when Jessica was in mid-adolescence that she gradually pulled away from her. She felt relieved when she was accepted by a prestigious college. She continued to study and enjoy intellectual pursuits after she got there.

Although Jessica didn't feel "too happy" at college, she did fall deeply in love with a young Jewish man (she had been brought up in the Episcopalian church) and her love was reciprocated. Their relationship was stormy, characterized by many fights, particularly over the question of commitment; specifically, could he settle down with her and get married or was he too confused? Finally they broke up because he couldn't make up his mind. Ironically, years later, she felt this same question was bedeviling her present relationship, but this time she was ambivalent.

As we worked together, I started to understand her confused feelings. First, her mother had a vested interest in discouraging the notion that a man could be trusted as a lifetime partner because it would then call into question her own decision to divorce her husband. The mother would respond in a snide fashion when Jessica and her sisters began discussing their various boyfriends in the presence of their mother. Rarely could a boyfriend pass muster.

Second, because her parents stopped getting along when Jessica had reached early adolescence, an impressionable age, she felt pessimistic about whether a woman could count on a man. Her own father had started to drink and became quite hostile to his wife just when Jessica herself became interested in boys.

Last, Jessica had a lonely childhood because of all the family moves and because of her competitive relationship with her sisters. In all, she found it difficult to believe that she would ever find relief from depression or loneliness.

Gradually I understood that my role as therapist was not just to help Jessica make sense of her childhood and its relation to her present-day life but also to help her form enough of a social network so that she would no longer be so terrified of depending on one person. Further, after I understood that her boyfriend was a decent, intelligent man who would make a loving husband and father, it was my job to keep her from fleeing him out of a misplaced fear that she was condemned to replicate her mother's fate. Gradually, she found herself more comfortable relying on me in the therapy and on her boyfriend, friends, and relatives outside of the therapy. Her hypercritical tendencies toward everyone including herself softened. She ended up getting married, and we stopped meeting for a time. Jessica later returned to therapy to talk over a variety of life decisions. After she had her first child, she told me "I never realized how lonely I was all the time. Now I hardly ever feel that sense of empty despair and when I do it shocks me."

Jessica's story illustrates that while a therapist investigates how fears from the past keep a patient from properly assessing people in the present, the therapist's job also includes helping the patient take preventative steps to make sure that she doesn't keep repeating the behavior that leads her to feel depressed and lonely. Thus, when it looked as though Jessica was going to break up with her present boyfriend even though she couldn't think of any really valid reason to end the relationship, as her therapist I had to take a clear position that I thought doing so might be a mistake.

It is too easy for therapists to become so involved in the mystery of understanding the past that they forget the job of helping the patient to insure that his future is not so isolated and objectively depressing that a relapse becomes likely. Any medical or therapeutic intervention is a three-part process: assessing the present symptoms; using some form of treatment to "cure" them; and finally, figuring out how to prevent the same symptoms from recurring.

If we dwell for a moment on the third part of a therapeutic intervention—how to prevent a relapse of the symptoms—we discover that there is some controversy about the best way to accomplish this goal. Some researchers feel that depression is an illness which can be described as a "kindling phenomenon." This phrase implies that each time depression occurs, its occurrence in the future becomes more probable because (for reasons we don't yet understand) certain patterns in brain response seem to become more deeply encoded with repetition. These researchers contend therefore that those who have needed antidepressants to alleviate several episodes of depression ought to stay on antidepressants indefinitely to prevent rekindling.

Other psychiatrists, who have been called "pharmacologic Calvinists," are opposed to leaving a patient on psychoactive medication indefinitely. These practitioners periodically take their patients off medication while helping them develop alternate "natural" ways to stave off depression. Membership in a rich social network is one effective natural antidepressant. We will be discussing the formation of a social network in detail in some of the subsequent chapters.

Mihaly Csikszentmihalyi, a professor of psychology at the University of Chicago, describes a second kind of "natural antidepressant" in his book *Flow: The Psychology of Optimal Experience.*[7] Csikszentmihalyi has devoted three decades to studying the details of what produces a feeling of contentment. In the course of his research, he has found that those people who report the greatest contentment often pursue one or more activities that lead them to become oblivious to the passage of time because the effort involved in mastering the activity is so gripping. The activities that lead to the greatest contentment incorporate two key elements: they provide a source of feedback that lets the participant know if she is succeeding and they involve the opportunity to progress to the next level of difficulty. For one person, taking piano lessons might fill the bill (the teacher and the student's ear provide feedback and the student moves on to more complex pieces as her skills improve), while for another collecting rare butterflies might do the trick.

Csikszentmihalyi contends that when faced with empty stretches of time, most people will naturally start to experience worrisome, insecure thoughts which eat away at their self-esteem. Thus, he feels it is vital to have a portfolio of creative activities that can be used to stave off the emptiness and fretfulness that come from not having enough to do or from a sense of purposelessness.

Therapy provides the patient with the leisure to mentally meander through dreams, wishes, and topics of curiosity. As a result, therapy allows the patient to discover and experiment with new "flow" activities which have the potential of serving as natural antidepressants. Even though we emphasize throughout this book the importance of forming a social network which can act as a buffer against future depressions, it is vital to remember how effective many solitary creative activities can be in keeping depression at bay.

Melanie, Dr. Jacqueline Olds' patient, is a good example of a lonely woman who finds solace in her own creative activities. She also wants more connection with others but realizes that she needs a context to stay connected.

Melanie is an graphic designer at a major university who is thirty-six years old and married without children. An attractive woman who wears handmade jewelry and elegant clothes, her eyes were filled with pain when she first consulted with me. She cried often and easily in each session although neither she nor I could always fathom what she was crying about. Gradually it emerged that Melanie had almost no social contacts outside of her husband. She had broken off entirely with her parents some eight years ago and had gradually descended into a full-blown clinical depression affecting her sleep, her appetite, and her energy level. After Melanie started an antidepressant medication she regained her appetite and ability to sleep. Her facial expressions became more animated, and she became a fascinating storyteller in her therapy sessions. Her artistic talent emerged as she revealed that she secretly dreamed of an art career.

But Melanie still lived in a tiny social world. She felt that her parents, and in particular her mother, were too crazy for her to resume contact without risking her sanity. She told stories of growing up in her parents' world (her mother is Armenian, her father Danish) in which they lived a largely isolated life with their four children in a well-to-do suburb of Philadelphia. She felt her parents were "house-poor" because as her father had succeeded at his accounting work, he bought a huge house for his family which left them no money for luxuries or even college educations.

Both parents managed to convey to their children that life is basically hellish and that you should not expect too much. The mother's depressive point of view was accompanied by a judgmental and grandiose outlook that made Melanie feel that she could never get a grip on whether she was devoid of talent or the artistic heir to Picasso. Melanie's lack of clarity about what she was like had dogged her since high school when she retreated from socializing with a group of friends, opting instead for a cocoon-like relationship with her boyfriend.

Although she broke up with that boyfriend, her pattern of living had been established and her marriage fit on the same template.

Unfortunately, Melanie's lack of social connections outside of marriage put a tremendous strain on the marriage itself, which was part of the reason for her depression. She felt that she and her husband were chronically estranged even though he was supposed to be her closest intimate.

Melanie complained that she got along well with her fellow workers, but that she froze inside as soon as someone made an overture to get together after work hours; she refused all offers and invitations. In my office she confessed that she was sure she would run out of things to talk about after the first few sentences. "Nothing ever happens to me," she said sadly.

Meanwhile, I was impressed by her interesting conversation ranging from art to politics and food. It was clear that Melanie was determined to squelch all social overtures for fear of anyone recognizing how colorless and lonely she felt. Only within the context of psychotherapy could she admit how sad and lonely she was used to feeling; this frankness then allowed her to become the scintillating conversationalist she truly happened to be.

During therapy, Melanie took up metalwork as both an art and a craft. She began designing her own brand of fine jewelry as a side business to her regular job as a graphic designer. Since the department in which she worked had about 150 employees, Melanie and a co-worker decided to hold a Christmas craft fair to sell their artwork. A friendship developed between the department members participating in the event. Melanie came to appreciate how comfortable she could feel when she worked on a project with other people.

Unfortunately, after the craft fair ended, Melanie felt she could not deal with the friendship without the glue of a mutual project. She lapsed into her previous role at work, socializing while at the office but not letting anyone get to know her much better outside of it. Although we are still working on this issue, it is clear that Melanie needs to bring several ongoing joint projects into her life in order to feel less lonely because she does so much better at socializing when her role is clearly defined.

During her therapy I strongly encouraged Melanie to resume contact with her parents, which she did. I had noticed that in most cases, no matter how difficult the parents might be (as long as they weren't criminal in some way), the toll taken on a person who cuts off communication is almost worse for the child than for the parents themselves.

It seems that we all have a notion of how things ought to be, and for most people this includes maintaining contact with those who are biologically responsible for our birth. No matter how peculiar or incorrigible our parents are, we all tend to feel much more part of the human race if we are at least on speaking terms with them. Although at times Melanie still feels antisocial and depressed after resuming contact with her parents, her depression does not have the same immovable quality that she had experienced earlier; the episodes were much shorter.

As we evaluate the potential of psychotherapy as a possible cure for loneliness, we recognize our own ambivalence. Indeed, for two of us psychotherapy constitutes our livelihood and our calling. Having placed our bias on the table, we offer some general observations.

First, therapy is one of the more obvious and frequently used solutions applied to the problem of loneliness and depression in contemporary America. But we contend that rather than being a cure, this reliance on therapy may be an additional pathological product of our culture's emphasis on *self-sufficiency*.

We feel that therapy may be overused on occasion; people sometimes fool themselves into thinking that it will decrease the overwhelming anxiety and hard work involved in forming or increasing a social network. Although therapy (and sometimes medication) may decrease anxiety, the work of initiating social contacts still remains, even after a productive therapy experience. In truth, the job may be greater than before the therapy began because for some patients the gratification of "being themselves" in therapy is so great that they neglect their everyday relationships.

We must also reiterate that a therapeutic encounter is not a good blueprint for healthy everyday relationships because it lacks the give and take implicit in normal healthy friendships, even though therapy gives the patient the feeling of relief that comes with speaking openly. Many of us are in the habit of assuming that it would be a misuse of our closest relationships to "impose" our troubles on friends and relatives. Fearful of being a burden, we worry that no one would like us if we revealed our unhappy feelings.

In reality, friends and intimates start to feel peripheral if they can never really be of help with the life issues that matter most. So in the end, as therapists, we worry that patients' "real-life" intimate relationships can become depleted and devitalized through lack of use, much the way a muscle atrophies when deprived of regular exercise.

However, when a person has grown so depressed or isolated that he cannot reconnect on his own, therapy does have the capacity to give him a jump start. It can do this in a variety of ways. First, thinking aloud in the company of the therapist allows a person to begin to deal with areas of his life that may have been left fallow simply because they were not being discussed.

Second, as the patient and therapist reconstruct the patient's life story, the patient can begin to recognize and understand the impact of some of the automatic habits he has acquired that may drive people away.

Third, as he develops an understanding of the way his early life with his parents and siblings affects the person he has become, he begins to shed the feeling all young children have, which is that they are helpless, events happen, people are arbitrary, and none of it makes any sense. As he learns more about the distortions carried into the present from childhood, he gradually finds that his once automatic reactions become more a matter of choice than lock-step reflexes.

Fourth, through therapy, the patient may come to appreciate the pleasure of talking honestly about himself. With luck a ripple effect will occur in which the person strives to be more true to himself in his real-life relationships, but these relationships will also be enhanced by a give and take that provides balance and completeness over time.

# 5 Medicines, Drugs, and Loneliness

As we struggle to overcome our loneliness and isolation, drugs have come to play an increasingly important role, whether they are prescribed in doctors' offices or purchased on the streets or in package stores. In the process, the drugs themselves begin to change our social world.

## Office Drugs

One of the most remarkable achievements of modern psychiatry is the discovery of medications that effectively treat depression and dramatically restore a depressed person's connections to the world. Depression shatters connections. A depressed person is cut off from family and friends, from the satisfactions of work and the pleasures of recreation, and from the world itself by a peculiar unresponsiveness to its changes and possibilities. At its worst, that disconnection can be made permanent by suicide.

Anxiety too can become an impenetrable barrier that isolates an individual from the surrounding social world by infusing each encounter with feelings of dread, a pounding heart, and the desperate wish to be somewhere else. Medication can play an important role in lowering that barrier as well.

Medication then can help restore our connections to one another and make life less lonely. At the same time, our society's increasing use of medication may be reshaping our social world so that "unmedicated" involvement with others becomes, for many people, even harder than it used to be. The changing social expectations that accompany the widespread use of psychiatric drugs can make the struggle against loneliness even harder for those who are naturally withdrawn and choose not to "treat" their condition with medicine. We will explore both these aspects of the use of medication in the treatment of depression and anxiety.

Thomas, a thirty-eight-year-old married father employed by a university science laboratory, went to the university health service at the insistence of his supervisor. With a long record as an effective technician, Thomas now seemed distracted, apathetic, and unproductive. He was referred to Dr. Schwartz, who became his psychiatrist.

When Thomas first entered the office he moved very slowly. His face was impassive, his voice monotonous, as he described a wreck of a life. He was unable to work, he said, but even if he could, he felt his job was pointless. Furthermore, there was no love between him and his wife; they might as well be living in separate worlds. He perceived his children as merely irritants, demanding attention that he had no wish to give them. He wondered about suicide, or at least a divorce, a way to escape his family. He reported that several trials of antidepressant medications over the years had made no difference at all. His life was an angry failure and he saw no hope of change.

Since Thomas had a history of thyroid disease, which can sometimes look like depression, I called his internist to check the results of some thyroid tests. She told a very different story from the one Thomas related. Yes, he had been depressed before, but antidepressants had produced an astonishing effect. When taking them, he was like another person—cheerful, engaged, and enthusiastic. Thomas's certainty that antidepressants could not help him was just another bleak distortion in his thinking caused by his current depression.

I told Thomas what his internist had said and that I wanted him to resume taking a medication called nortriptyline that had worked well for him in the past. He was not at all pleased, but agreed to take the medicine. He managed to convey his disdain, letting me know that he would go along with my request just to show me I was a fool.

Within weeks Thomas was dramatically better. His movements were animated, his face and voice expressive. His concentration and energy came back and he found that his interest in his work returned. He felt like himself again. He spoke of his family with warmth and love, describing his wife as a wonderful person. He was no longer heading toward an embittered loneliness, cut off from those he had loved. And, once again, Thomas made clear that I was a fool—this time for having listened so seriously to his complaints about his wife, when I should have understood that they were just symptoms of his depression.

Obviously, there is a good deal of complexity to this story. By asking if Thomas was correct in his final assessement of his situation, we ignite a passionate debate between two camps of "true believers": those who hold that the primary causes of depression are biological and those who believe equally strongly that psychological causes are primary. Were Thomas's bitter complaints about his job and family just symptoms of an altered biological state, or were they real feelings that he pushed aside until they overwhelmed him in a debilitating depression?

One thing was clear, however. Thomas had spent most of his life productively embedded in the dual worlds of work and family until he felt powerfully estranged from both by depression. It is also clear that antidepressant medication reestablished his connection to his work and revived his sense of loving involvement with his wife and his children.

A similar argument can be made about the use of medication in alleviating certain anxiety disorders. Panic disorder with agoraphobia, for example, is a dramatic affliction that leaves patients subject to sudden attacks of terror characterized by symptoms including feelings of imminent doom, breathing difficulty, racing heart, sweating, and shaking. In a desperate effort to avoid the attacks, people begin to restrict their activities, sometimes to the point of becoming "housebound." Social phobia, another anxiety disorder, is an extreme version of the uneasiness that many of us feel in unfamiliar social situations. It too can lead some patients to drastically restrict their lives.

Curiously, while "antianxiety agents" (especially some of the newer relatives of Valium) can be helpful, panic disorder and social phobia often respond remarkably well to certain medications developed specifically for their antidepressant properties (such as Prozac and its relatives). These antidepressants have pharmacologic effects that are very different from those of conventional antianxiety medications. In other words, drugs developed specifically as antidepressants have unexpectedly shown themselves highly effective in the treatment of some anxiety disorders.

To see how medication can help overcome anxiety, let's look at the experience of another one of our patients. June was a forty-year-old married mother working as a legal secretary when she first came to Dr. Richard Schwartz for treatment.

June had her first panic attack in her early thirties while driving alone on a snowy highway. She was forced to pull over to the side of the road until the feeling of panic passed. Over the next few years, the attacks occurred regularly whenever she traveled alone more than five miles from home. June found the attacks to be almost unbearable and the only way she knew to control them was to avoid the settings that triggered them.

Consequently, she began restricting her travel and narrowing her world. She even left her job so that she could take a position in an office located near her home, on a familiar route that still felt safe to her.

Before the onset of the panic attacks, June had felt tied in to an extensive network of friends. Always fearful of another panic attack, she stopped visiting those friends who lived outside the "safe" zone. She also limited visits to relatives to times when her husband could accompany her.

June entered treatment feeling that her previously full life, rich with friends, had become pitifully impoverished. She was gripped by a powerful loneliness that she had not known since her childhood. A low dose of an antidepressant medication prevented the occurrance of further panic attacks. Psychotherapy helped June understand the complicated feelings she had about some of her relationships and helped her risk reentering the world.

Once again, we see medication dramatically restoring someone's ability to be engaged in the world and involved with other people. When we recall the findings about social networks and health that we examined in chapter 3, we see that these medications offer not only the direct benefits of relieving depression or anxiety, but also the indirect health benefits that come from creating or renewing social connections. Just as strong social networks can play a role in shielding us from depression and anxiety, antidepressant medication can help us modify our social world in ways that decrease the likelihood of future depression and anxiety.

A complicated interaction begins to develop, however, between our use of medication and the social perspectives that support its use. In America today we frequently resort to medicines to treat increasingly mild forms of anxiety and depression, conditions that would not have been considered "illnesses" until recently. Furthmore, we are finding that the medicines are often highly effective. This discovery is at the core of the "Prozac debate." It is essentially an argument about how far we should carry psychopharmacologic treatment into the realm of "normal" human experience.

We will concern ourselves with one small corner of the debate: the effect these new developments in psychopharmacology have on how we understand loneliness (both as individuals and as a society) and what we do about it. Therefore, we must turn our attention from the role of medication in the treatment of devastating disorders that shatter our connections with those around us, to the use of medication in reducing the more "ordinary" experiences of unhappiness and isolation. Greg's story provides insight into this area.

A successful entrepreneur who started his own lumber company and made it grow, Greg eventually sold his business to a large corporation. At forty-seven, he suddenly found himself a millionaire in retirement. Greg had lived his whole life in the small city where he was born. He married his childhood sweetheart and together they had three children, who were teenagers at the time he came to therapy. While success sometimes isolates a person from former friends, Greg's business success had served to strengthen his ties to the community. He was frequently sought out to serve in volunteer and charitable organizations.

Freed by his early retirement, Greg and his wife made a critical decision. Wanting the best possible education for their children, they moved from their hometown in the Midwest to Boston. That move introduced the "ordinary" American experience of dislocation and loneliness into an extraordinary American success story. One year after the move, Greg still felt vaguely depressed, yet manifested none of the other symptoms that would lead to a psychiatric diagnosis of depression. Still, he had made no new friends, involved himself in no new projects, and spent much of the day sitting alone and reading. A low dose of Prozac changed all that. He roused himself, began to investigate community organizations in his new city, and gradually began to devote both time and money to his church and to an organization that taught farming and gardening skills to inner-city adolescents. Through these activities, Greg began to develop new friendships and found that he was once again a meaningful part of a community.

Looking back, this basically shy man realized that he had felt most "himself" when his leadership role in his company provided an orienting context for his day-to-day dealings with people. By contrast, his wife's experience was very different. More naturally outgoing, she had quickly developed a network of friends and volunteer activities in their new community.

Greg's shyness was not a problem for him as long as he lived and worked in a community where he was known and respected. When he left that community behind, his shyness was just enough to prevent him from creating a new set of relationships. Prozac provided a jump start, probably by producing a mild elevation of mood and a slight decrease in social anxiety. Given the social realities, Prozac was a godsend. But there are other possible social realities, including the one that Greg left behind. He had no need for Prozac as long as he lived in a community where his neighbors actively sought to include him in their projects, instead of his having to seek out opportunities to join in with people he barely knew. The point here is that we are fast becoming a country where shy people like Greg are more and more likely to find themselves needing a little help from Prozac.

We live in a society that no longer reliably provides us with a stable social network: a sense of belonging that grows automatically from the places we live, the families we are born into, the occupations we pursue. If we are to be part of a social network, we (like Greg after his move) must often *do* something to find it, to connect to it, even at times to create it. We can no longer count on family, work, and neighborhood, what the sociologist Brigitte Berger reviewing a book on the homeless for the *New York Times* called those "mediating structures that alone have the capacity to provide lonely individuals with a stable anchorage."[1]

Our society rewards outgoingness not only with career success, as it probably always has, but with a social inclusion that, until recently, depended little on personal initiative. Individuals who are shy, who are uncomfortable with change and novelty, who at other times would have been carried along by the relative stability of social bonds, are in trouble. On one level, Peter Kramer's book, *Listening to Prozac,* is the story of a drug that allows those of us who are temperamentally shy to make the social connections that we all need. (It is important to interject a cautionary note, however. Antidepressants like Prozac certainly do not "cure" all shyness. They are however a step in that direction for at least some individuals.)

Harvard professor of psychology Jerome Kagan has undertaken meticulous long-term studies of innate temperament, observing children both in America and abroad from infancy into adolescence. His work shows that about 10 to 20 percent of all infants are born with a tendency to be significantly shy.[2, 3, 4] Their physiology makes them less able to adapt to new stimuli, new situations, and new people. While their temperament is not a fixed destiny (many of these children do indeed become more comfortable over the years), it certainly is an added burden, particularly in modern America.

This leads us to something of a dilemma. It would be good news indeed if medications could reduce the type of social anguish experienced by 10 to 20 percent of our population. The bad news, however, is that the very success of that treatment encourages us to accept the continuing evolution of our social structures in ways that increase the likelihood that a significant number of people will experience loneliness in the absence of medication. By chemically altering individual social styles, psychiatric treatment supports and strengthens a social system that might otherwise warrant change, a system that simply does not meet the needs of a large segment of its population without pharmacologic assistance. Consequently, we are in danger of neatly sidestepping the option of actively working toward social changes that can lead to more stable and inclusive community bonds. Such bonds would reduce the pressure on all of us to behave in an outgoing, socially interactive manner that was alien to Greg's nature but came easily to his wife.

Now, easy sociability is not a *bad* thing. It is no less "normal" and certainly no less desirable than mildly depressed reticence. Similarly, most of us would find a traditional role-bound society, one which would not allow Greg and his wife to relocate in search of better opportunities for their children, far less appealing than a society that allows each individual to forge his or her own arrangements anew. The latitude to redefine our lives goes hand in hand with the American dream of freedom and opportunity.

The crucial point is that we are dealing with a relatively new and remarkable circular interaction between a culture and its psychopharmacology. If a medication can make people less shy, we start to expect shy people to take their medicine. We become less willing to adjust to their shyness. Shyness is recast as an illness to be treated, rather than part of the range of ordinary human foibles. A new medicine permits us to make our social norms more rigid.

This same interaction between medication and social expectations is vividly illustrated by the use of antidepressants in "normal" grieving.[5] It offers us a clearer view of where the social use of medication can take us. A group of psychiatrists at Yale studied the treatment of "depressions of bereavement" with antidepressant medication. They prescribed antidepressants to individuals who seemed to linger in a depressed state after the death of a spouse and found "preliminary evidence for the use of antidepressants in treating the persistent major depressive syndromes observed late in the course of bereavement."[6] In other words, antidepressants helped those widows and widowers who remained depressed long after the death of their spouse. That's good news, but what do the researchers mean by "late in the course of bereavement"? The authors do not specify the duration of bereavement in their sample, but the introduction suggests that they are concerned with depression that persists one year after a loss.

A strikingly divergent view of bereavement may be found in British psychoanalyst Anthony Storr's book *Solitude*. Storr emphasizes that certain psychological processes simply require time for their completion, sometimes a lot of time. In rural Greece, widows mourn for five years. During that time, the grieving woman wears black, makes daily visits to her husband's grave, and conducts graveside conversations with the departed.[7]

Storr quotes from anthropologist Loring Danforth's study, *The Death Rituals of Rural Greece*: "A new social reality is constructed which enables the bereaved to inhabit more fully a world in which the deceased plays no part.... The process is brought about through a gradual reduction in the intensity of the emotions associated with death, through the formation of new social relationships with new significant others, and through the constant confrontation with the objective facts of death, climaxing in the exhumation of the bones of the deceased. The result of this process is as complete an acceptance of the final and irreversible nature of death as is possible."[8]

We will sidestep the sexual politics suggested by the apparent absence of a similar extended ritual for widowers in rural Greece and immediately agree that, as clinicians, we were delighted to learn that antidepressants offer another treatment option for patients who are trapped in the pain of unresolved grief. Even so, we have an interesting situation. Our culture expects that normal grieving will be a relatively short process. Naturally, there are individuals who cannot conform to cultural expectations. We can now bring their grieving to an end "on time" with antidepressants. Medication can be used (and we are sure will be used) to support our cultural expectations about normal mourning. Any pressure to reconsider those norms will be further reduced because psychopharmacology can make it possible for more of the population to conform. We have a circular interaction in which cultural norms elicit pharmacologic interventions which in turn reinforce cultural norms.

A similar dynamic is possible in our efforts to offer pharmacologic help to people who are shy or socially ill at ease or a little lonely and sad. As psychopharmacology permits a larger proportion of a population to fit within the bounds of cultural expectations, those expectations become narrower, more uncompromising, leading in turn to an even greater need for pharmacologic intervention. The result of this process is twofold. There is a decrease in the misery that comes from a poor fit between temperament and social structures. One can also predict a decrease in society's tolerance for individual differences in temperament and the corresponding range of responses people experience in the face of trying circumstances. While Greg is happier, we all become a little less tolerant of people who do not "get out there" to make new connections. The pressure to reshape our communities so that shared tasks bring people together as a simple fact of ordinary life becomes a little less compelling.

As doctors, we welcome any approach that extends our capacity to relieve the suffering of our patients. As citizens, we worry about the direction in which, taken collectively, all those individual and humane acts of prescribing may lead us.

## Street Drugs

Of course, Prozac is not the first drug that people have used to ease their way into social encounters. Our traditional remedy has been alcohol. We have built many cherished social customs around the use of alcohol as a "social lubricant." In recent decades, other drugs, particularly marijuana and cocaine, have competed with alcohol for this role in certain groups. Are Prozac and its relatives (a class of medication called *selective serotonin uptake inhibitors*—SSRIs) any different from these nonprescription remedies? Do they carry with them any distinctive implications for our society or will they simply be absorbed into our existing quandary about "street drugs?"

Fran Leibowitz, an iconoclastic trendsetter on the New York publishing scene, contends that the social class of the user is the only difference between office drugs and street drugs. From her perspective,

> "Every middle-class person in America is on Prozac. Every poor person in America is on crack. Every middle-class person who is on Prozac has tremendous contempt for the poor person on crack. Yet it's the exact same thing. In fact, there is much more excuse for the poor person to take crack. But the motivation is the same...Only a moron would not be depressed."[9]

Of course, Leibowitz intends to be provocative, but her choice of crack cocaine as a foil to Prozac allows her to offer an oversimplified analysis in terms of social class. If instead we compare Prozac to alcohol, which does an excellent job of spanning the social spectrum, we must acknowledge that cost and availability are not the only differences between "recreational drugs" and antidepressants. There are also differences in their effects. One of the most important has to do with what a colleague of ours, Robert Aranow, has called the principle of Conservation of Mood. The principle is expressed as follows: Any substance that induces an elevation in mood above an individual's normal long-term baseline will eventually result in an opposite equivalent or greater decline.[10]

Essentially, the principle makes explicit centuries of experience with "mind-altering" drugs: any improvement of mood that they grant us is extremely short-lived and comes at the price of increased depression down the road. Prozac has created such a stir in large part because it seems to violate the principle of Conservation of Mood. It is therefore a hands-down winner (at least in pharmacologic terms) for reducing the depression of everyday life.

When it comes to managing ordinary social anxiety and easing our way into social interactions, the gap narrows a little. The biggest pharmacologic difference is that recreational drugs are intoxicating. They produce a "clouding of consciousness" that is not compatible with high-level, efficient functioning in a variety of tasks. So alcohol "works" at parties but not in the workplace. But now, even at parties, Prozac is becoming a pharmacologic alternative for some people who are uncomfortable with alcohol's intoxicant effects.

Ellen, a middle-aged woman who was not depressed but who began taking Prozac in an unsuccessful effort to lose weight, described its effects in words strikingly similar to what is often said about having a drink or two: "I used to be uncomfortable with strangers at parties, but now I can go up to anyone and say anything I want to. Also I am more decisive and people say I am more attractive."

The role of alcohol in social interactions and social structures has received much attention over the years from historians and sociologists. Their observations can help us understand the use of the range of substances now available to make it easier for us to connect to others.

Alcohol has played an important role in almost all cultures, but it may have a particular function in modern, individualistic societies. In a lecture delivered in 1944 at the Yale Summer School of Alcohol Studies, the sociologist Selden Bacon examined the use of alcohol in "simple" and "complex" societies and concluded that we have an increasing need for alcohol to promote "social jollification." Bacon defined complex societies as cultures transformed by specialization, a process that carries with it fragmentation into separate social groups, the rise of individualism, and a shift to a money-based economy. In a view remarkably consistent with the picture we have painted thus far, he contended that specialization leads inevitably to an increase in the importance of drugs like alcohol in promoting connections between people:

> We have, on the one hand, a society whose individuals are often (a) more self-contained and independent, (b) more ignorant of each other's interests and activities, (c) more separate from each other, and (d) more prone to aggressive and competitive relationships; on the other hand, there is a need for unsuspicious, pleasant, relatively effortless joint activity [to maintain social order and unity]...

There is also the need of the individual to make contacts, both occupational and recreational. In a specialized, competitive world, recreational devices for the individual seem more essential. Yet the factors just discussed make difficult the attainment of that easy, trustworthy, noncompetitive friendship situation which is requisite for interpersonal relaxation. Alcohol is obviously functional for achieving the lessening of suspicion, of competitive tension, of the barriers usually present between strangers in our society.[11]

In our specialized, mobile society, with few shared tasks or shared experiences, most of the people around us are strangers. Loneliness may or may not be one of the causes of alcoholism, but it certainly makes the use of *some* alcohol more likely in order to ease the awkward first overtures between individuals who share little beyond the wish not to be alone. The danger of using alcohol in this way is that people then find it hard to believe that their comfort with each other can be sustained without its ongoing help. We turn again to one of our patients to illustrate this point:

Paul's connections to other people were always a bit tenuous and uncomfortable. He felt that even these connections were slipping away. An engineer in his late fifties, he faced a forced early retirement. He and his wife had drifted apart over the years, each devoting their energy and attention to different sectors of life. Their sexual relationship had ended long ago, against his wishes. Four children were all that linked husband and wife together and gave Paul some sense of purpose in his life.

When his youngest daughter graduated from college and moved away, Paul felt completely cast adrift and terrified by his aloneness. In his despair, he found a remedy. A few drinks in a shady bar helped him to feel sufficiently relaxed and engaging to enjoy the attention of a "hostess" and to believe, if only for a little while, that she genuinely cared about him. The outcome was never sex. The sexual overtones excited him, but what he treasured most were simple words that kept his loneliness at bay.

A fascinating fact about alcohol these days is that not only does its use enhance the ease of socializing, but ceasing to use it also opens up unique possibilities for connection. Alcoholics Anonymous offers recovering alcoholics a safety net enjoyed by almost no one else in this country—a guarantee that, no matter where they are, no matter what time it is, they need not be alone. It provides them with a ready-made social network characterized by remarkable generosity and resilience in an otherwise fragmented world.

We will talk more about AA in the chapter on self-help groups, but in considering drugs and loneliness it is important to identify the two interventions found to be most effective in treating alcoholism—AA and family therapy. Both of them rework and restore the alcoholic's social ties. AA's importance was described movingly by a sixty-year-old man who participated in a longitudinal study of Harvard graduates that extended from college into old age. He spoke several months after joining AA but was still an active member two years later.

> Most alcoholics, I believe, grow up in a glass isolation booth which they build for themselves to separate themselves from other people. The only person I ever communicated with was my wife. AA shows us how to dissolve the glass walls around us and realize that there are other people out there, good loving people.
>
> I love the AA meetings and love being able to call people when I feel tense. Occasionally, someone calls me for help and that makes me feel good....I wish there were some form of Alcoholics Anonymous for troubled people who don't drink. We old drunks are lucky.[12]

We might add that many of us who are not troubled but simply lonely, living in a world with many glass walls, might also envy this "old drunk."

# 6   The Small Group Phenomenon

If the antidote to loneliness is companionship, what better place to turn for solace than to one of the thousands of small groups that meets regularly throughout the country? When people join small groups, they often say they do it because they are looking for community. According to sociologist Robert Wuthnow, director of the Center for the Study of American Religion at Princeton University, four out of ten Americans belong to a small group "that meets regularly and provides caring and support for its members."[1] They take many forms: twelve step programs, Bible study groups, parent groups, singles groups, and groups devoted to a wide variety of special interests. Most of the people who regularly attend these gatherings report that the experience has improved the quality of their lives. Some have overcome enormous difficulties while others describe more general benefits, like making new friends.

We believe that small group participation can indeed offer relief from loneliness and isolation, but we add a note of caution. One can choose among numerous groups to join and some are more effective than others in helping form the kind of relationships people usually yearn for when they complain of loneliness. Much attention has been given in recent years to the burgeoning variety of active self-help groups. But other groups also deserve consideration, including those that relate to religious fellowship as well as those groups formed to meet the specific needs of people drawn together by a shared interest or life circumstance. Let's begin our exploration of the options by taking a look at the self-help groups and the recovery movement in general.

Launched in 1935, Alcoholics Anonymous (AA) is structured on a series of twelve steps designed by founder Bill Wilson and his colleagues to enable group members to control their addiction to alcohol. AA has given millions of alcoholics the support they need to recover. Through their participation in AA, many of these people have found the success that eluded them when they tried to quit drinking on their own, resorted to antidepressants, or tried psychotherapy.

According to Dr. Donald Nathanson, senior attending psychiatrist at the Institute of Pennsylvania Hospital in Philadelphia, "These people are almost intractable by conventional methods but if you group alcoholics together, they know each other's tricks, they begin talking about them, and they begin to heal each other."[2] The guiding principle of AA, as expressed in its preamble, is to "stay sober and help other alcoholics to achieve sobriety."[3] AA groups do not permit participants to interrupt, advise, or question one another.

AA has changed over the past decade, as a result of the baby boomers' enthusiasm for the growing recovery movement. Some of the old-timers observe that today's new members are less interested in reaching out to fellow alcoholics than in using the meetings to call attention to themselves. At the same time, other long-term members welcome the new participants, saying that they enliven the movement by talking openly about relationship issues once considered private.

Veteran AA members tend to resent youthful newcomers who behave as though the meetings are a social event, not a twelve step program. Today nearly half of all AA members are between the ages of twenty-one and forty and nearly one-third are women.[4] Old-timers sometimes sense that the baby-boomers who flood their meetings are self-involved and that most are eager to find an audience to whom they can parade their pain. Instead of talking about alcohol, they divulge difficulties with their lovers, fears about job security, and the pain their parents have inflicted on them. This change in attitude is associated with the fervor of the recovery movement as a whole, fueled by the works of popular gurus like John Bradshaw, who contends that 96 percent of our population belongs to a dysfunctional family.[5] What Bradshaw is actually saying, of course, is that the dysfunctional family is the norm, a proposition with which we cannot agree.

Today dozens of other programs replicate the twelve step approach, using it to solve a broad variety of problems reflected in the names of groups like Workaholics Anonymous, Anorexic Bulimics Anonymous, Nicotine Anonymous, and Debtors Anonymous. An additional set of groups helps friends and relatives of people who suffer from these problems: Adult Children of Alcoholics, Co-Dependents Anonymous, Families Anonymous, and Alateen, among others. People seek to recover from just about every malady modern life has to offer, from overeating to overshopping to overexercising.

In addition, many of us identify ourselves as the victims of every kind of affliction from incest to battering to psychological abuse. There are so many self-help groups that a new organization has emerged whose sole purpose is to help organize data relevant to the self-help movement. The National Self-Help Clearing House provides contact information on all types of groups. Yet while the groups have proven useful to many participants, they do have their detractors.

Psychologist Stanley Katz, coauthor of *The Codependency Conspiracy,* questions the value of twelve step programs for relationship issues and other behavioral problems. "It's like using penicillin for every disease," he says. "AA was developed for alcohol....But many people go to meetings for the social life or because they have other problems they're trying to cure on a free basis."[6]

Katz contends that the widespread application of the disease model—labeling dozens of maladies as illnesses—allows people to view themselves as unwitting victims and to shrug off responsibility for their own behavior. Many people subsequently become dependent on the programs they attend, caught up in the seemingly endless cycle of being "in recovery."

We sympathize with Katz's point of view and, in fact, we see this book as something of an antidote to the codependency movement championed by writer Melody Beattie, author of the best selling *Codependent No More.* Beattie uses the term "codependent" to describe how people with low self-esteem invest themselves in filling their partner's needs while ignoring their own.

Although many people certainly do get caught up in this dynamic, we think there are many others who find it a convenient rationale for an overdose of self-involvement. Once we stop feeling sorry for ourselves and bemoaning the difficulties and demands we have endured, we can get on with the business of achieving healthy interdependence—that splendid state in which one willingly accepts comfort and assistance and just as eagerly gives it to others.

In our view, the way to escape the misery and isolation that evolve from codependency lies not in self-involvement but in extending one's universe. When we stop focusing on ourselves so intensely and start to ask what contributions we can make to others, we can begin to enjoy new relationships and the promise they hold. Certainly self-reflection and the cultivation of an inner life are important, but when such contemplation becomes all-consuming it prevents us from moving on.

Sometimes we need a group of people to nudge us to get moving and there are many to choose from besides the twelve step programs. Support groups designed to confront a specific life dilemma can be extremely practical. A good example is groups that are designed to help those who have lost jobs to cope with the emotions unleashed by unemployment and also with the logistics of finding a new position. Discussions center on issues like how to sell yourself, restructuring your resumé, and how to find unadvertised job opportunities.

While participation in such a group doesn't alleviate the financial problems intrinsic to job loss, it does provide relief from anxiety and a place where members can vent the fear, frustration, and shame associated with unemployment. They can do so without either loading their problems solely onto their families or closing themselves off from their loved ones by refusing to even acknowledge the problems. Dr. Barrie Greiff, coauthor of "The Psychosocial Impact of Job Loss," notes that mutual support can dissipate the stigma and isolation of job loss.[7]

Spouses of unemployed men have also started to form their own support groups, where women talk about their financial fears, how to alleviate their children's worries and embarrassment, how to help their husbands cope when they slide into depression, and how to deal with people who go out of their way to avoid the subject of unemployment.

As one woman confided to us, "When your husband loses a job, some people act as though someone has died. They don't know what to say so they start avoiding you, which makes you feel that not only has your husband lost his job but you're losing your friends, too."

Our national crusade to solve social problems through participation in self-help groups has, however, escalated to the point where some people now question whether it infringes on our civil rights. Courts frequently route those arrested for DWI (driving while intoxicated) into AA programs by offering offenders the choice of a lengthy license suspension or participation in a treatment program. Similary many states allow doctors and lawyers with substance abuse problems to enter such programs instead of having their professional licenses revoked.

Harvard Medical School senior research associate Archie Brodsky and psychologist Stanton Peele write in *Reason* that "Prescribing treatment as a substitute for normal criminal, social, or workplace sanctions represents a national revision of traditional notions of individual responsibility. When called to account for misbehavior, the criminal, the delinquent teenager, the malingering employee, or the abusive supervisor has an out: Alcohol (or drugs) made me do it. But in exchange for the seductive explanation that substance abuse causes antisocial behavior, we allow state intrusion in people's private lives. When we surrender responsibility, we lose our freedom as well."[8]

To compound the situation, there is also some doubt as to the effectiveness of treatment when a person joins a program only to avoid a stiffer punishment.

Other critics of the recovery movement believe that self-help groups thrive partly because they fill the gap left by the absence of the extended family structure that used to thrive in many American communities. Unable to meet all our needs within the confines of the couple relationship and the nuclear family, we resort to self-help groups to fill that void.[9] Yet there are other ways to approach this problem, ways which do not require posing as victims. While there is nothing wrong and indeed much right with seeking a broader circle of companions, we think there is much to be said for joining or forming a group predicated on the notion that each individual is committed to a *group* task rather than one that casts its members as victims who seek purely personal relief from the suffering of a dysfunctional family environment.

We human beings are very susceptible to social pressure and, once we see ourselves as victims, we fashion a set of expectations that limits our experience within that group to just those feelings, activities, and discussions concerned with being a victim. When we seek membership in a group in order to enrich our lives and those of others, we ignite a cycle that awakens our strengths and challenges us to bring forth our best.

Certainly twelve step programs have proven enormously helpful to millions of people, succeeding often where conventional therapy has failed. However, the tendency to overprescribe worries us. By superimposing the AA model on dozens of other problems, we dilute its effectiveness. While antibiotics are powerful, miraculous medicines, they do not cure all our physical ills. Neither can we expect the tenets of the twelve step programs to alleviate all our emotional anguish.

Most self-help groups including the twelve step programs are grounded in a spiritual ideology. Some self-help models are authoritarian, claiming that there is only one way to solve a problem. People are taught that they cannot stop their addictive behavior by themselves. The belief that they can manage without the group is treated as just another symptom of their addiction. Recording her observations of participants in codependency groups, Wendy Kaminer, author of *I'm Dysfunctional, You're Dysfunctional*, notes, "They are encouraged to see themselves as victims of family life rather than self-determining participants."[10]

The first step in twelve step recovery programs is admitting that you have no control of your addiction and that you cannot will your way to improvement. The next step is giving yourself over to God's care.

Even though it is called a self-help movement, the recovery approach can encourage us to feel incompetent. When we are labeled as adult children, for example, we are encouraged to shed responsibility for our actions. We become invested in our own suffering and we learn to wallow in self-pity. Furthermore, as we explore intimately the wrongs that have been inflicted on us, we sometimes trivialize the harm inflicted on others. As Kaminer explains, there is something qualitatively different about growing up in a series of homeless shelters compared to coming from a family where your parents continually bickered about bills.

"The selfism of recovery is more a failure of community," she writes. "At least it reflects a very shallow notion of community, which is not a group of people going on about themselves in the belief that they're all equal in their pain. Community requires an awareness of inequalities, the desire to correct them, and faith in your capacity to do so."[11]

Unlike the consciousness-raising groups that emerged during the early years of the feminist movement, the recovery movement has no political agenda. While women used those earlier groups to explore personal issues related to growing up female, they did so in the broader context of a social movement designed to create political change. Members wanted to change both the psychological treatment of women and the way they are treated in the workplace. The interplay between the intimate and the public aspects of feminism nourished the sense of community that developed among women involved in these groups. In contrast, when members of the various survivors' groups and twelve step programs testify about their experiences, they seldom cry out for the kinds of social reforms that could strengthen the family and reduce the tensions and ignorance that are often at the root of the very abuse they have suffered.

We offer these observations not to dismiss the recovery movement, for certainly it has brought comfort to many. Yet it is important to exercise caution. The further the twelve step approach wanders from the original type of problem it was designed to address—alcohol addiction—the more questionable its application. We can indeed learn invaluable lessons from those who share our painful experiences, but the question is whether those lessons are best learned in the format of a twelve step program. There are many other types of groups to choose from, some formal and others informal.

Before immersing yourself in a twelve step program, consider carefully the kinds of changes you hope the group will help you to make in your life. If your primary goal is to manage a specific addiction, such a program may be an intelligent choice. If your goal is to become more involved in relationships characterized by warmth and reciprocity, which will help you feel more connected and less lonely, this may not be the best way to do it. Indeed, if your purpose is to make new friends, there are certainly other venues to explore.

We do not need to label ourselves as victims in order to deserve and enjoy the camaraderie of small group participation. There are hundreds of groups to join (and hundreds of others waiting to be formed). And while some groups discourage community by channeling participants into focusing on themselves, others encourage it by placing the emphasis on helping one another grow or by embracing a task or mission that extends beyond the walls of the group.

As we have said before, the key to overcoming loneliness lies in connecting not only with individuals but with people who share a vision and who are ready to work together to achieve it. Overcoming loneliness implies psychological growth. It implies exposing your feelings and thoughts to the scrutiny of other people and taking some emotional risks. It means making a commitment to working through the inevitable kinks that develop in the process of living a life that benefits the community as a whole.

The rapid proliferation of small groups in this country can be partially attributed to the increasingly fractured, anonymous, hurried nature of contemporary American life. As we have previously noted, the hunger for community is rooted in the dissipation of both the nuclear and the extended family and in the increase in mobility that characterizes our society. Small groups are created with the specific intention of soothing those very real feelings of displacement and disconnection, and in this respect they can be viewed as reviving community.

At the same time, because of their episodic nature they fail to replicate the sense of belonging we have lost. Attending weekly meetings, dropping in and out as one pleases, shopping around for a more satisfactory or appealing group—all of these factors work against the growth of true community. "Community always lies at the intersection of individual needs and institutional structures"[12] writes Robert Wuthnow in his book, *Sharing the Journey: Support Groups and America's New Quest for Community*. He cautions us not to expect more of these groups than they can deliver:

> "When I say that the small-group movement is effecting a quiet revolution in American society, therefore, I mean that it is adding fuel to the fires of cultural change that have already been lit. The small group movement may be providing community for people who feel the loss of personal ties and it may be nurturing spirituality in an otherwise secular context. But it is not succeeding simply by filling these gaps. It is succeeding less because it is bucking the system than because it is going with the flow. It does not offer a form of community that can be gained only at great personal or social cost. Instead, it provides a kind of social interaction that busy, rootless people can grasp without making any significant changes in their lifestyles."[13]

## Choosing a Group

We have seen that small groups vary considerably. We have also seen that such groups affect the greater society in both positive and negative ways. Taking these observations into account, here are a few guidelines to keep in mind if you decide that you would like to become part of such a group. Our first word of advice is to be bluntly honest with yourself and to consider carefully just what it is you hope to get by becoming part of a group. Are you looking for help in solving a specific problem? Do you seek support in coping with emotional pain or an important life change? Do you hope to meet new people and make friends? The way you answer these questions can help you find a group that fits.

If, for example, drinking or drug use habits are disrupting your life, you may well feel drawn to a twelve step program where you will be in the company of those who share and understand your problem. If you are curious, attend a meeting or two simply to listen. Keep in mind that different chapters have different personalities and that while you may feel out of place in one group, another may strike you as more comfortable. One of the virtues of such groups is that you need not commit yourself to membership. If you don't like it, you leave. Of course, this fluidity is also problematic because it means that you can escape instead of wrestling with the very issues that brought you there in the first place. But, if you view the voluntary aspect of attendance positively, we think there is nothing wrong with doing a bit of prospecting. The idea is to make a suitable choice before you commit, so that once settled, you will attend regularly and make a commitment to being part of the group.

Many who shed their addictions with the help of AA report that their social lives become increasingly intertwined with other members of the organization. They attend meetings and social events together, offer support between meetings, and find that they begin to let go of some of the relationships which existed before they joined. If you join such a group, take care not to lose track of any positive relationships you already have, because if you neglect them and allow the support group to become the all-consuming center of your life, you will have squandered precious connections that are hard to restore.

Just as no one individual can completely satisfy another person's needs, neither can one type of relationship. Try then to choose a group that provides the opportunity to work on your difficulty but does not become so consuming that you cut yourself adrift from the other parts of your life. As we explained in our earlier discussion of the role of psychotherapy in alleviating loneliness, it is important not to neglect relationships which lie outside the therapist's office. Similar care needs to be taken when one becomes intimately involved with a group.

That said, we do need to add a caveat. It is sometimes necessary for a person to separate totally from old acquaintances in order to take control of an addiction. The alcoholic contractor whose social life revolves around the group of friends he meets at the local bar after work each evening may need to remove himself completely from that milieu in order to combat his addiction. Participation in AA extricates

him from a troublesome social network and replaces it instead with a
new one in which drinking has no place, a network which supports
rather than sabotages his efforts to quit drinking.

Sociologist Robert Wuthnow makes it clear that the self-help
organizations compose an important but numerically minor part of the
small group movement. He cautions us not to equate the movement
with networks that provide significant emotional support designed to
help members cope with serious personal crises. He adds that while the
large majority of small groups are involved in offering some sort of
support, most "are also devoted to the more ordinary desires for
community that the average American faces routinely. And most are
attempting to fill these desires through activities that are quite
commonplace, such as eating together, singing, praying, and talking. It
is not so much the activities that are changing American culture as the
way in which these activities are organized. The shopping around, the
emphasis on fitting in, and the fact that these activities may be
substituting for more traditional expressions of family and spirituality
are having the greatest impact on society."[14]

Sometimes people form groups because they feel distanced from
an institution but committed to maintaining their spirituality and
traditions. Throughout the country, groups of Jewish families have
gathered togethered informally to celebrate Jewish holidays and traditions outside of the structure of temple membership. Such groups are
known as *havurot*. While some of the families involved may retain a
connection with a temple, many do not. Some distance themselves
because they cannot accept the temple's attitude toward women, while
others, such as partners who are of different religions, find the havurot
a more comfortable setting in which to introduce their children to
Judaism.

The members of one New England havurot worked together for a
year to prepare for the bas mitzvah of the first child in the group to come
of age. Together they researched and prepared the music. The child and
her parents wrote the service, incorporating traditional Jewish prayers
with passages of their own making. This havurot gently blends social
awareness with religious observance, reflecting the attitude of its

membership. After a Passover service on a local beach, for example, the families spread out to clean up trash. They then decided that each family would write a letter to their local legislator urging passage of pending legislation involving the cleanup of local waters.

Kim, the mother of four daughters, has also used the small group format to satisfy her spiritual needs, but she has done it within the structure of the church. Her husband and children are not interested in being part of a religious institution, but Kim grew up with the church as an integral part of her life and feels she needs a connection even though she doesn't consider herself particularly religious. She solved her dilemma by joining the Women's Fellowship ten years ago, when she was in her mid-thirties.

"I don't attend services regularly," she says, "but I'm a member of the church and I'm a member of the fellowship." The group consists of about thirty women, ranging in age from thirty up to ninety-two. They meet regularly once a month, to participate in either an educational seminar or a social program. They also assemble as needed to provide refreshments after funeral services or for celebrations honoring the accomplishments of church members and their friends and families.

Kim explains, "We clean up the church when necessary and if there's a need for a piece of equipment, say a dishwasher for the kitchen, we'll raise the money to buy it. We also prepare dinner for a local soup kitchen once a month. Sometimes we're called upon to help out with children's activities or we might be asked to arrange a reception. When I was hospitalized for a long period of time, the fellowship organized a food chain and delivered a home-cooked dinner to my family every evening."

While Kim enjoys participating in the programs and helping those in need, she readily acknowledges that the companionship of the women involved draws her to the group. "These people have a lot of advice and experience to offer," she observes. "It's like doing something with your sisters, your mother, your grandmother. We share a lot of laughs and we all like helping people, but it's a real low-pressure situation. We don't have an agenda and there aren't any big egos involved. Everyone just accepts you."

If your primary reason for seeking a group to join is to make friends, choose one that attracts the kind of people you are likely to enjoy spending time with. Ask yourself, what kinds of things do I want to talk about, what kinds of activities do I want to share with these new friends I hope to make? If you want to chat about your family and find other moms and dads with whom to share the adventure of raising children, you will probably fare better by exploring a family fitness program at the local Y or a school organization, than by joining a recovery group.

Similarly, if your goal is to meet other single men and women, joining a singles group may seem the obvious answer but there are are other routes that can be equally successful. You might opt instead for a group that devotes itself to a cause in which you believe. In the singles group you are sure to meet other single people. But in the bird-watching group, the amateur theater company, the neighborhood improvement group, or the political action committee, you will meet people who share your concerns and interests and are willing to explore them together. Some of them may just turn out to be single, but even if they aren't, you have begun the work of creating a social network.

The friends you make working to stage a block party or to clean up a vacant lot in the neighborhood may eventually lead you to other people—some perhaps single—who share your interests and values. The idea is to choose a group that appeals to you because of the way it works, the values it embodies, and the activities it undertakes rather than because of the contacts it may afford.

Of course, you can always initiate your own group. This is a particularly effective route to alleviating loneliness and isolation for those who know people with whom they would like to socialize but seldom see because of the demands of family, work, and otherwise frantic or incompatible schedules. If your friends always seems to have other commitments, create a commitment that gets all of you together. For a couple, this might involve organizing a once-a-month supper club with a few other couples. Or you might follow David's example and launch a group to meet a specific need that manifests itself at the moment.

David was in his mid-forties when Jonathan, his longtime friend and neighbor, split up with his wife after nearly twenty-five years of marriage. When Jonathan moved to an isolated cottage about forty minutes' drive from his former home, David and three other friends worried about him and recognized that they weren't seeing much of him anymore. "Someone suggested we go up there and have a poker game and check him out," David recalls, so they did. From that first visit, the men started gathering monthly at the cottage. Jonathan, who loved to cook, would make dinner. After that came the poker. Then, barely a year later, Jonathan died.

"At his memorial service, we talked about whether we wanted to continue gathering," David says, "and we decided we did." That was six years ago. Now there are seven members in the group, including the original four. As a sort of tribute to Jonathan's memory, dinner remains an important part of the evening.

As David explains, "The host makes a best effort to put on as fine a meal as he can. The first time someone served cold cuts, an unwritten rule was broken. The next time that person made a very fine sauce." Another unwritten rule is that group members do not have their spouses prepare the meal ahead; they are expected to do it themselves. "Cooking and eating take up half the evening," David explains, "and the poker is really incidental."

Although the poker playing is low stakes and strictly amateur stuff, the card playing is not an attraction to David. He finds the evening becomes less pleasant once the game begins. And yet, he recognizes that it is an integral part of the group's ritual. Like many enduring groups, this one has developed its own lore, which tends to bind the participants together over time.

"There are two games we played up at Jonathan's cottage that were hilarious," David recalls, "and we tell the stories about them a lot. At the first one—this was such a great bunch of cardsharks—we couldn't figure out which direction to deal. So we carved an arrow into the table to show which way so we wouldn't forget. Another time everyone kept getting straights. We finally realized we were using a pinochle deck. It's almost primal, sitting around the table telling the same stories."

For David, who commutes an hour to work each day and seldom socializes, the group is vital because it keeps up his contact with men he likes and whose company he enjoys. "It's the only time this group of guys gets together," he says. "We're not a huge group and we're not a support group. We talk about work and we talk about literature because we all read. We hardly ever talk about women. There's a lot of affection at the table, and a lot of very different personalities. Everyone is pretty funny."

Although he sometimes misses several months in a row, David feels his loyalty to the group is unwavering. He says, "I'll never sever my relationship from this group, because of Jonathan. For me, the group is still tied up with him. He was the catalyst. When he died, there was already some cohesion."

Some groups are born when people experience a life change that separates them from those they are accustomed to interacting with on a regular basis. Sophie, a freelance writer, belongs to a "writers' group" composed of ten women who work as writers or editors. The group was organized fourteen years ago by a woman who had just left her job as a newspaper reporter to have a baby and begin a freelance career. Feeling professionally isolated, she called others involved in writing—a romance novelist, an environmental writer, a medical editor, and two all-purpose magazine journalists—and invited them to meet for lunch to share some shop talk. The group, which originally met every other week in a restaurant, now meets once a month in a member's home. Over the years, fifteen women have belonged. There are currently nine members, including the woman who initiated the group and three of the other originals.

Sophie explains, "We're pretty relaxed about bringing new people in. If someone wants to join, we run it by each other before inviting her to a meeting but I don't think we've ever said no to anyone. And then it's kind of self-selecting. The person will either like the group and come back or she'll be bored and disappear."

Unlike some writers' groups, in this one members don't read each other's work. Sophie said, "We talk about what we're doing, but we don't operate like a workshop. We go around the room and each person talks about what she's up to, and some of the time it's only vaguely related to writing. A few years ago, when a lot of us had small children, we spent a huge amount of time discussing how to find time to write. Now we give each other ideas about how to get work or market what we've got, but we also spend a lot of time just talking about politics, schools, our kids, whatever. I think that's why a few people dropped out. They wanted a tighter format, more focus on the writing. Some members talk about really serious things happening in their lives—like losing a parent or a serious illness in the family. Others don't. But the atmosphere is pretty supportive when people do want to talk about their troubles.

"I don't find the group too important anymore in terms of my career," she continues, "but I like the mix of women and there are several I never see except within the context of our meetings, so I keep going back. It's nice to sit around and share a bottle of wine with them and hear about what they're up to. Also, we're real loose about attendance. You don't have to be guilty about missing a meeting, so long as you let the hostess know, which makes it easy to drop out when you're busy and drop back in when you've got the time again."

Still other groups form in direct reaction to a specific situation. Nancy Berchtold of Yardley, Pennsylvania suffered severe postpartum emotional problems following the birth of her daughter in 1983. Two years later, her friend Jackie was hospitalized with similar problems. When Jackie thanked her profusely for being an understanding listener, Nancy decided to start a support group for women with postpartum disorders.[15] She advertised the first meeting of Depression After Delivery in her local newspaper. She and five others soon met in her living room. They voiced feelings they had never expressed before and quickly discovered that they no longer felt alone. Today there are one hundred DAD support groups.

When their wives joined a consciousness-raising group in the mid 1970s, Dick and three other men responded by starting a men's group. Twenty years later, the woman's group has long since disbanded but the men's group, which has grown to eight members, continues to meet once a week.

"We sit down and go around and check in with each other, see what's going on," Dick explains. "We don't have any sort of agenda, but through the years there have been periods where we've been deeply involved with certain issues. People tend to talk through decisions they're in the process of making. When I was thinking about leaving my teaching job, I spent a lot of time talking about that in the group. And we tend to talk about our kids and what they're going through."

Although Dick sees all of the men in the group socially outside of the weekly meetings, he explains that the men's group sessions are even more meaningful than just a gathering of friends. "I think what makes them different is the level of intention in terms of engaging around certain issues. People get pretty revelatory and they get a lot of feedback about where they're at. Also, there's an expectation of confidentiality, that certain things aren't to be shared outside the group, not even with the wives."

Having shared his life's journey from his thirties into his fifties with his men's group, Dick takes it for granted the group will escort him into his sixties, seventies, and beyond. "Recently," he says, "a couple of members have had fairly serious illnesses and we've found ourselves starting to talk about aging. I anticipate we'll be doing a lot more of that in the future."

As these examples show, small groups vary enormously in structure, purpose, and even size. Some are very formal and others are very loose. Some address a problem or fulfill a need while others focus more on camaraderie for its own sake. All of them offer a sense of belonging and the opportunity to get to know a group of people over an extended period of time. The type of group you choose will be determined by availability, your own initiative, and an honest assessment of just what it is you hope to accomplish through your membership. Finding a comfortable, productive situation may take time, but as we have seen, the effort may well be rewarded with the formation of satisfying relationships that last ten or twenty years, and even longer.

# Part 3

# How to Make Connections

# 7 What to Do If You Feel Single, Lonely, and Friendless

"I can't stand the thought of being alone all weekend."

\* \* \*

"I feel like such a fraud, pretending to be normal and happy at work, when really I just dread going home because there's no one there and I've got nothing to do except watch TV and fall asleep."

\* \* \*

"I think I've lost the knack of talking to people and socializing because I'm so used to being alone."

These comments have a familiar ring. Most of us have had similar thoughts at one time or another in our lives. We hear these words frequently, voiced by by our patients and friends, men and women who appear outwardly as though they have adjusted well to living alone.

In reality, their chronic state of isolation leads them to feeling awkward and ashamed. Most of them do all they can to consciously conceal their loneliness, motivated by the fear that other people would be repelled if they knew how desperate they felt.

Living alone is a skill that takes time to develop. For those who had companionship most of their lives, it requires learning to do things in a way that often feels unnatural. Most people who have learned a way to manage living alone get "set in their ways," as we used to say about older widows and widowers, spinsters, and bachelors; they do not lightly risk changing their state because it took so long to master. But because our society puts such a high value on relationships, many solitary types feel embarrassed about what they consider to be a pathological style of life that they have adopted by default.

One of the central themes we want to emphasize in this book is that some of our cultural values compound the difficulties of being alone at the same time that they propel us toward a greater likelihood that we will end living by ourselves. The beliefs that need highlighting include both the push to look and act as self-sufficient as possible and its corollary: "If I'm lonely there must be something wrong with me since no one else seems to mind doing things alone."

Essentially, this second belief leads many people to pretend that loneliness is not a problem and that they really like doing things by themselves. (Partly because they have become such good actors, others assume they don't mind being alone.) Because this value is often internalized early in life, some people feel that they are better human beings when they can appear to be self-sufficient. They take bittersweet pride in not asking favors of others and they begin to doubt that anyone would be willing to do them a favor if indeed they did ask. Predictably, an unhealthy self-centeredness can develop in the most normal people if they find themselves isolated over time with no one to offer feedback or an alternative perspective.

The important point is that in the ordinary course of life everyone has to go through periods of being alone. Sometimes one is alone when leaving college and finding a first job in a new city. Or a corporate move may offer no alternative but resettlement in a new location. Sometimes one is alone after a divorce or the death of a spouse. Unfortunately, we live in a culture which encourages people to take pride in being self-sufficient and at the same time makes them feel ashamed of feeling lonely and needy during isolated times. Once we realize the pernicious effect these values have on normal adult development we can turn our collective backs on them and instead be more honest with ourselves and others.

How would "more honest" play out? Before going to a party peopled by strangers, "I've got to do it on my own" would be replaced by "I hate having to meet people on my own. Do you think you could keep me company?" Faced with living in a new neighborhood where no one is familiar, "I'll have the post office hold my mail while I'm away" would be replaced by "I'd be so grateful if you could pick up my mail while I'm gone." Only by consciously making ourselves aware of the myriad situations in which we assume that the proper way to behave is to be fiercely independent, will we be able to stop ourselves from discouraging the offers of help that could eventually lead to friendship. Let's take a look at how Anne was able to overcome her problem with loneliness.

Anne Miller, a twenty-six-year-old graduate student at a major Boston university, lives with her fiancé in student housing along the Charles River. Anne spends a great deal of time alone in their apartment doing homework and "puttering about" because her fiancé's library job keeps him out very late at night. While alone, she often gets extremely panicky, fearing that some criminal will try to enter the apartment and attack her. There are in fact more break-ins along the river than in other parts of the city.

Anne began therapy with Dr. Olds to seek relief from her panic episodes. Medication immediately eased her anxiety and the focus of the sessions soon turned to the way her life is organized. The possibility of inviting fellow students over for company while she studies was discussed. Anne also noted that her parents live in a nearby suburb but that she didn't want to burden them with what she considers foolish worries.

In therapy Anne confessed that she misses her mother immensely and acknowledged that her mother always seems grateful to see her. It was soon agreed that she should spend at least one evening each week at her parents' house. She decided to study at the library on the other evenings, using the university shuttle service for transportation so she wouldn't have to walk alone in the dark. This plan considerably reduced the time she spent worrying alone and put her in a good position to deepen her relationship with her parents and study partners.

The relief Anne experienced once she felt released from the need to "prove" that she could manage her weekday evenings alone was palpable. She was soon able to discontinue therapy while maintaining the program of low-dose medication and "structured" evenings that reduced her time alone.

Thus we see that the first order of business in living alone is to retrain our thinking so that we no longer invest enormous energy into fooling ourselves and others into believing that doing things alone is terrific and that we don't need anyone else's help or companionship. Further, we should recognize that we have plenty of company when it comes to pretending that we are content to be alone. Then we need no longer feel ashamed of either our loneliness or the lengths we go to conceal it. If we can stop blaming ourselves for being alone and feeling lonely, we can then channel our energy into finding something to do that makes rumination (obsessive repetitive thinking) less likely.

In researching his book *Solitude*, Anthony Storr reviewed the biographies of many philosophers and writers who lived extraordinary lives devoid of the intimate relationships of marriage and parenthood that are commonly considered a requirement of healthy adjustment. Writing in defense of the solitary lifestyle, he says, "Our expectation that satisying, intimate relationships should, ideally, provide happiness and that, if they do not, there must be something wrong with those relationships, seems to be exaggerated." He goes on to remark, "It may be our idealization of interpersonal relationships in the West that causes marriage, supposedly the most intimate tie, to be so unstable. If we did not look to marriage as the principal source of happiness, fewer marriages would end in tears."[1]

Storr reminds us not to ask too much of our intimate relationships and, in his tales of solitary creativity, reveals the value of solitude. His biographies of genius do not, however, provide easy lessons for more ordinary lives. The work of Mihaly Csikszentmihalyi,[2] a University of Chicago psychologist mentioned earlier, fortunately offers a practical bridge between Storr's inspirational stories and the aloneness that we must all face from time to time.

He makes the point that everyone, no matter what their psychological background, becomes worried and fretful and feels insecure in the face of large amounts of unscheduled time. If you start to feel worried and sad when you are alone with nothing to do, do not assume that your feelings are rooted in some terrible character flaw or some dark secret concealed in your past. It is true that being with someone else often has a mind-focusing effect that makes fretfulness a little less likely, but it is also possible to reduce the anxiety and sadness associated with loneliness by yourself. This can be achieved by cultivating a repertoire of "flow" activities, which so strongly engage your creativity that you become oblivious to the passage of time.

One of Csikszentmihalyi's most interesting findings indicated that while most people naturally assume they are happiest while on vacation, when researchers actually "sampled" their mood states over time, these same people usually rated their level of contentment greater when they were immersed in their usual work. Having interesting activities that grip us, whether they are part of our work or an avocation, makes us more content and less vulnerable to periods of plummeting self-esteem.

If you are experiencing a solitary period in your life, the next problem you face is not wanting to try new things alone. Many lonely people respond to well-intentioned suggestions—that they join an exercise class or volunteer to help out with a community project, for example—by automatically saying, "That's just not something I could try on my own." Yet the sad irony is that by avoiding new experiences, you deprive yourself of the opportunity to begin forming a social network so that you will know people with whom you can do things in the future.

If you can overcome your antipathy to taking a risk, chances are you can think of someone else who shares your plight and who would love company in trying something new. If, however, no one comes to mind for the activity you want to try (for example, joining a neighborhood association or a yoga class), you may have to figuratively jump off the high-diving board and try the activity on your own.

Your new involvement may well provoke high anxiety the first few times you venture out, but soon it will become more familiar and less threatening. As time passes, a happy anticipation will probably emerge from the haze of anxiety. In the course of your adjustment, you will begin the process of making friends without making a self-conscious effort.

## The Process of Making Friends

Let us remind ourselves how this "making friends" business actually happens. First, we should bear in mind that the usual spark that ignites friendship is the regular interaction provided by a common task. Second, for most people the prime time for making friends occurs in school or college. Involvement in an intense work situation (for example, nurses working together in an emergency ward) can also fuel friendship. Sharing a similar stage of life, such as the childbearing years, is also conducive to making friends.

The thread that unites all of these situations is the existence of a common experience: as students, as coworkers, as parents. In all these experiences people lean on each other just to get through them (borrowing each other's notes in school, taking care of each other's children). Such situations frequently produce long-term friendships just because the effort they require often leads people to temporarily shed their inhibitions about dependency.

The challenge is to create similar opportunities to nurture friendships during the phases of life that do not supply them automatically. The trick for the single person is to find a way to meet enough people involved in a similar phase of life. At the same time, you purposefully involve yourself in joint tasks with people you could potentially like. When you do that, making friends is likely to happen on its own as long as you are willing to let others get to know you. It can also help if some of these joint tasks incorporate the expectation that participants will lean on each other for help or support. Alcoholics Anonymous is a stellar example of an organization that utilizes this principle.

Many AA members who have not only given up alcohol but who have also made very good friends within the organization report that the regular meeting times and the concept of the sponsor (a person who is both a guide and someone you can call any time, night or day, if you feel tempted to go back to drinking) are some of the reasons that AA is so successful. In fact, AA is a wonderful blueprint for the things a group can offer its members; unfortunately, it is also an example of one of the many groups in our culture that requires its members to be addicts or victims in order to qualify.

The question arises, "Where do I turn to find people going through my phase of life who might be interested in a common project task?" One can begin by recalling a familiar experience in college. You can remember making friends with several people in your dorm. At first you may have thought the match was unlikely but often these same people turned into lifelong friends. The lesson here is that when seeking potential friends or partners for joint projects, it is worth looking in your own backyard or neighborhood. The convenience of geographic proximity increases the probability that, once formed, a relationship will survive. (If you are truly surrounded by people with whom you can't imagine sharing *any* activities, it doesn't hurt to contemplate relocating to a more compatible neighborhood.)

When asked to imagine an ideal living situation, most of us envision a group of trustworthy, likable neighbors with whom we can at least exchange favors and at best entrust with our personal secrets. Although much has been written about the demise of the neighborhood, many people in America wish to feel close to their neighbors. Certainly there are also those who purposefully avoid becoming too familiar with others on their street or in their apartment building ("Good fences make good neighbors"), but we think this is the exception rather than the rule. We will have more to say about the nuts and bolts of making a neighborhood work in a later chapter.

Another good place to search for candidates for shared projects is in an ongoing context such as work or school. These settings provide a continuing framework in which you can slowly get to know people. When you see the same people regularly, day after day, they gradually reveal their temperament and personality. This continuity gives you the opportunity to recognize those people you consider potential friends or companions.

The key notion here is that the ongoing context functions as an adhesive that holds the two of you together during the anxious period of getting to know each other. At this early juncture in a relationship, it is all too easy for one or the other person to get cold feet and give up altogether on the whole idea of getting closer. But because this shared world requires that you see each other regularly, there is no need to rush and no excuse to fall out of contact.

Why is this suggestion any different from the age-old advice for meeting new people that your mom used to give: "Why don't you join a church choir?" Actually, it's not so very different; we are instead trying to spell out some of the reasons mom's advice was on target. Our notion is that shared tasks and projects offer a solid opportunity to increase your social network. To make this happen, you need to involve yourself in an activity that is in itself so appealing that your enthusiasm for it will carry you along in the early stages of involvement, before friendships take off. If the activity or topic captures your imagination, you will probably be at your best rather than hopelessly self-conscious and awkward, as you might be if you were motivated only by the self-imposed mandate, "I've got to make some friends."

The mutual project can take a wide range of forms, from volunteer activities to craft cooperatives, political causes to theater groups. Do bear in mind, however, that some mutual activities are much more social that others. The people who sign up for ballroom dancing lessons or who join a restaurant sampling group are more obviously interested in making social connections than those who become involved in "Friends of the Harbor Islands," for whom the first priority is the conservation of undeveloped land.

This "motherly advice" has lost credence because lots of moms implied that joining up would reap an almost immediate crop of new friends. This is usually not the case. Disgusted and disappointed, many single people quit an activity after about six weeks. They regard their experience as a failure because they did not make any new friends. Realistically, it usually takes six months to a year of involvement before friendships germinate. That is why it is so important to join a group that focuses on a subject you find fascinating, preferably a "flow activity" (i.e., one which is so interesting to you that you won't notice the passage of time while doing it).

By involving yourself in a diversified portfolio of activities you can widen the circle of people from whom to choose a social network. At the same time, by pursuing a number of interests, you reduce the possibility of having a single activity grow stale. Take care though not to make yourself so frantically busy that there is no time for spontaneous social encounters should friendships develop beyond the context of the group.

Although many single people nowadays use dating services and personal ads in their search for romantic relationships, it is our hunch that these tactics do not lead to as many "good matches" as when people get to know each other gradually through shared tasks. Most people who succeed in finding love report that they did not know, on a first or second meeting, that they had discovered the person who would become central to their lives. Usually the attraction builds gradually as new facets emerge to create an increasing mutual interest—and then over weeks and months a slow dance of move and countermove often leads to the crescendo of a sexual encounter.

When an introduction comes from a dating service or a personal ad, there is tremendous pressure on both individuals to make up their minds fast since the sole reason for the encounter is to decide if they are romantically interested in each other. Without a context that holds people together over time and permits them to reveal themselves to each other in a relaxed way, someone is more likely to make a snap judgment based on anxiety or fear. For example, a woman might feel that a man she meets through a dating service is too aggressive sexually after a first date, but if they were in a class together, each would learn about the other in a less pressured way and know more about the other's natural level of reserve; thus, the man might be less likely to misjudge the woman's style and expectations.

Another pressure from dating services or personal ads is an atmosphere of "comparison shopping" which is not always conducive to romance. A women we know wrote a witty and engaging personal ad for *New York* magazine and received fifty responses in short order. She went out with twenty of the fifty men and found many of them to be interesting, decent individuals with whom she enjoyed spending an evening. In the end, however, she felt that none of them were worth pursuing and decided to place a second ad. We suspect it is hard to think or feel clearly when comparing twenty possible suitors with a bewildering array of attributes by sampling each of them for an evening, especially when you can't go to the public library and look them up in *Consumer Reports*. Joining groups that share a common task or interest and then "discovering" the appeal of someone alongside you is a much better bet.

Rachel, a twenty-seven-year-old Jewish woman who emigrated from England with her family four years ago, is a good example of a woman who understood the necessity of involving herself in group activities. She came into therapy with Dr. Olds because she felt intolerably anxious. A slim, attractive blonde who worked as an associate at a Boston law firm, she lived at home with her parents. She knew that most Americans her age didn't live with their families but she assured me that such an arrangement was typical in the Jewish community in London. Since her parents gave her as much privacy as she wanted and charged her no rent, she thought it was the best arrangement for now.

Rachel speculated that she had inherited an anxious temperament from her mother. In addition, she was terrified that she would never find anyone to marry. She felt that she hadn't been able to make true friends in this country because the people she met didn't share the cultural values that were integral to the close Jewish community in London in which she was raised.

She did think she had tried many realistic routes to meeting people and her therapist had to agree with her. She participated in Israeli folk dancing each week at Hillel, a club for Jewish college students. She belonged to the young professional branch of Combined Jewish Philanthropies and she attended some social evenings at a young Jewish professional group called the Tuesday Club.

As her therapy progressed, Rachel revealed that she had been unpopular in school as a teenager. The thought that she was essentially unlikable still haunted her. Specifically, it had been hard for her to be part of the "in group" of girls she admired, and no boys were interested in her. Now she felt as if all her acquaintances were gradually pairing off and that she was going to be left out in the cold.

She also feared she would turn out like her mother, whom she saw as too high-strung in her dealings with her children and husband. Rachel harbored terrible memories of her mother's chronic irritability. In contrast, she felt her father and brother had laid-back, playful personalities, and that things came fairly easily to both of them.

In therapy sessions, we were able to flesh out the pictures of her mother and father so that the mother wasn't always cast as the bitch opposite the father's saintlike role. As she came to see her mother in a kinder and more realistic light, Rachel's harsh judgment of herself seemed to soften. Coincidentally, her acquaintances in folk dancing started to become friends rather than competitors. Suddenly a man she hadn't noticed at the Tuesday Club started to express a real interest in her.

We thought it was likely that as she accepted her mother and by corollary herself, the barriers that prevented her from letting others get to know her in these groups started to fall away and suddenly her relationships began to deepen. Rachel was in the right position to make the most of her new insight because she had already put in her "germination time" in several social groups.

As you consider which groups to join, with an eye to choosing those whose activities will hold your interest over a sustained period of time, there is another important principle that your mother might have mentioned: "What you get out of something is directly proportional to what you put into it."

When we invest effort in an activity or project, even if we do it under duress—for example, KP at summer camp, an internship in medical training, boot camp in the armed services—we often look back on those experiences with a fond affection. We do so because of the relationships we formed during those times when we had to immerse ourselves in the work at hand. Similarly, those who work hardest to advance a particular cause, hobby, or business are usually the ones who are most likely to discover that they have also made some long-term friends. So if the group needs an officer, committee chair, or publicist, figure out if your skills match the position and if they do, volunteer to fill it.

Although most people who are shy feel squeamish at the thought of being president, treasurer, or secretary, it is often easier for a shy person to fill a position that gives structure to her group participation rather than to be just one more member without a clear role to play. Further, the position will encourage you to attend the group religiously (because you feel an enhanced sense of authorship and responsibility), which makes it more likely that it will eventually pan out in some good relationships.

As we think about "deepening" relationships we realize that eventually one person has to take the initiative to ask another person to do something apart from the group which has brought them together. Even before this happens one person has to learn enough about the other to choose a good activity for the two to share outside of their familiar context. Many shy or lonely people avoid going out on a limb and initiating a social encounter because they are so fearful of rejection. Often the unwillingness to take such a risk stymies their chances of allowing a relationship to deepen. Conversely, if one person ends up doing the lion's share of the "initiating," he may get burned out and feel that no one really likes him.

The concept of "exchange theory" emerged from an anthropological study of Pacific island cultures (Polynesia and New Guinea). In the words of anthropologist Bradd Shore, civilizations there seemed to rest on "reciprocity; an almost mystical obligation a gift imposed on its receiver to make a gift in return."[3] Whether people exchanged pigs, shells, or food, the exchange (either immediate or delayed, in the manner of the San people of the Kalahari) became the medium through which social connection was sustained. It seems to us that our modern equivalent of the gift is asking someone to join us in an activity or a meal.

Unfortunately, instead of regarding shared activities and meals as "gift-equivalents," which offer the opportunity for reciprocity, most of us think of ourselves as either "initiators" or as people who wait for others to call. This self-categorization often means that the people who do the waiting can be left out of the reciprocity loop altogether unless by some improbable chance they link up with someone who doesn't get depleted by constant initiating. (This dynamic, of course, is not so simple when it involves two people of the opposite sex looking for romance. In this situation, depending on each person's age, a set of rules governing dating traditions may come into play.)

If you try to think of someone initiating an activity with you as the equivalent of a gift, it may seem more natural to pay them back in kind. But just as you might not reciprocate a gift if you want to discourage a relationship from developing, failing to ask the other person to join you in an activity might well be construed as a signal that you are not interested in pursuing the relationship.

Unfortunately, this odd aspect to our culture—namely, the vagueness of rules regarding reciprocating invitations—means that some people might not immediately understand the signal. Therefore, this whole cycle of "giving a signal" by not reciprocating sometimes has to happen several times before it is read correctly. We will disuss this further later in the chapter.

### Facing the Long Weekend

It is very easy to feel discouraged and depressed when the week is coming to a close and you have nothing to look forward to. There is the inexorable sense that everyone else has social plans, that you are the only person with nothing to do. As one woman describes her Friday afternoons at work, "I creep around feeling invisible while I listen to little snatches of conversation about this party or that movie the people around me are planning to go to."

Persons who feels isolated and out of the social loop may find it hard to remember how it felt when they were included. They may also wonder how they ever got in the loop in the first place. Ironically, for many people brought up in middle-class settings, the end of childhood marks the disappearance of a comfortable niche in which social events seemed to occur with no planning whatsoever. In reality, much of that seeming comfort can be attributed to mothers who worked overtime to plan social gatherings for their children. It may be that their efforts backfire because they do not allow their youngsters to get enough practice at initiating their own social events.

Are there some simple guidelines for dealing with the upcoming empty weekend, a situation which everyone has encountered at one time or another? One obvious principle is to seize opportunities to socialize that just happen to fall into your lap. Frequently an unexpected social occasion will arise that can relieve the emptiness of the weekend. Embrace it—even if it is not an activity you would have planned, even if you are feeling demoralized. The event may prove tedious, in which case you can always excuse yourself early, but it is also possible that you will encounter someone who interests you.

For example, many shy isolated people think of the holiday office party as the low point of the year. They foolishly assume that they are alone in their apprehension, but in fact, most people feel awkward about going to a social function in which none of the familiar rules regarding office behavior quite apply. If you go to the party determined to get to know the people who interest you the most, the occasion can serve as a structured way to deepen some of those office relationships without having to take a risk that might feel awkward during work hours.

Usually getting to know someone means asking enough questions so the person understands that you are genuinely interested in them. Some people think of themselves as social initiators who draw others out, while another set of people waits to be drawn out. The difficulty with this situation is that it may well lead to one-sided conversations that prevent relationships from taking off. So once again we need to emphasize the importance of reciprocity. Taken within the microcosm of conversation, it takes give and take to get a relationship off the ground.

The weekly softball game is an excellent example of an office gathering with the potential for increasing one's social network. Sue is an attorney employed by a nonprofit corporation that raises money for cancer research. She felt like an outsider at work partly because she was the only attorney employed by the organization and few people understood her contribution. She was also younger than many of the people working there and felt she was at a different phase of life. While many of her coworkers were either married or paired off, she had no significant other with whom to go to office parties or out to supper. Then she heard that many of the people she worked with got together informally on Friday nights at a local park to play softball.

Sue had loved athletics in high school, so she went to one of the Friday games to see what it was like. She found playing softball relieved much of the anxiety she felt about being at a different phase of life because she didn't have to make small talk. Before joining this activity she felt singularly inadequate when the conversation turned to children, houses, vacations, or investments. With softball, she could throw herself into the game and enjoy the people without feeling that she had to pretend to be something she was not, namely settled and committed. Because softball happened every week, she gradually became more comfortable with her coworkers. Soon she and the few other single people in the group started to go out for drinks after the game.

While the first guideline for dealing with an empty weekend is to seize the social opportunities that present themselves, the second is to recognize that the weekend is probably empty because you haven't made any plans. Some of us fail to plan because what we really want are rich, reliable friendships that yield plenty of spontaneous activities just when we want company. The fact is that most people aren't able to do things at the last minute because they are trapped in what Barbara Ehrenreich refers to as a "cult of busyness" in her book, *The Worst Years of Our Lives.*[4] In Ehrenreich's scenario, we compete frantically to prove our importance through our busyness.

Caught up in the cult of busyness, many of us orchestrate our lives so there is hardly any time available for socializing (which is a good defense for anyone who is scared stiff of loneliness). Once again it is hard to read the social signals correctly. When people turn down your invitation with the excuse they already have plans, it may mean that they have full rich lives scheduled in advance or it could simply mean that they are not interested in socializing with you. It is often necessary to give people a few opportunities before you can be sure which is the case. "Miss Manners," Judith Martin, eloquently discussed the difficulties involved in properly reading social signals in one of her columns:

*Dear Miss Manners,*

*In cultivating friendship in my small town where everybody sees everybody in passing, I have called folks who claim to enjoy my company and promise to call me soon. Then they don't.*

*This would be fine, if disappointing—I can take a hint and do not call them again. However, when next we meet in passing, months later, they invariably exclaim, "I've been meaning to call you but…" (fill in litany of ordinary, pressing and not-so-pressing tasks of daily living).*

*While I grant these folks' good intentions, their salutation implies the queasy suspicion that they are feeling more guilty than glad to see me. I feel I've become a pitiable case in their eyes.*

*Now, I would be happy to base our relationships on pleasant chats at chance meetings, but their opening line makes further talk seem a cover for their omission, and so detracts considerably from my pleasure in conversation. Please advise me of a rejoinder respectful of both me and them.*

*Gentle Reader:*

*While she has no desire to make excuses for these people, Miss Manners does not necessarily assume that they intend to snub your social overtures. It is now common to live such a messily crammed life as to neglect social pleasures, as well as obligations, and their clumsy excuses may merely reflect their embarassment at having done so.*

*The reply that would save face for you, as well as for them, is a cheerful, "Oh, I know how it is, I've been busy too. But it would be fun to get together if we can manage it sometime." Acknowledging that busyness is merely the human condition, it nevertheless leaves open the possibility of their initiating sociability with you.*[5]

If it looks like you are going to have a lot of time to yourself over the weekend, try not to panic. Carin Rubenstein and Phillip Shaver, social psychologists at New York University and authors of *In Search of Intimacy*, offer some essential advice:

> When you are alone, give solitude a chance. Don't run away at the first sign of anxiety, and don't imagine yourself abandoned, cut off or rejected. Think of yourself as with yourself, not without someone else.

In concrete terms, this means doing some of the things by yourself that you enjoy doing with other people, whether that means listening to your favorite music, watching a video, or making a meal together. It is important to have something to look forward to, but the activity ought not depend on having another person present. We are astounded at how often the most lonely, depressed people lose the hang of being alone because they "forget" that there are some activities they enjoy for their own sake (for example, writing in a journal, going to the theater, visiting a flea market), with or without the company of others. They envision themselves happily enjoying a social occasion built around good food, entertainment, and music, but they overlook the potential these same activities hold for enhancing their solitary time.

Rubenstein and Shaver, discuss the difference between "sad passivity" and "active solitude." They characterize the former as including "sleeping, doing nothing, drinking, overeating, taking tranquilizers, watching television, and getting 'stoned' alone." They contend that when people start engaging in the activities of sad passivity, they become entrapped in "a downward spiral from emotional and social isolation to depression and illness."

"Active solitude" includes distractions that are pleasurable because they include some active engagement (like exercise, painting, golfing, or reading), as well as social actions in which a person takes steps to help others, either strangers or people they know, instead of sitting at home and feeling sorry for themselves.

From our perspective, asking and doing favors for people who seem like potential friends becomes a kind of social action, one that is very different from helping the needy or joining a sewing group. In its most basic form, it means being willing to borrow an egg if you are making a cake, without feeling that you are imposing. Each time you ask such a favor, you imply, "I would do the same for you next time." It doesn't hurt either to make this message explicit rather than simply implied. By overcoming the reluctance to ask favors that plagues so many of us, you can take the first step in establishing a social network rooted in reciprocity, with the eventual goal of making yourself matter in someone else's life.

Establishing a pattern of give and take in the context of daily routines is just as important to building community as joining a group of people interested in a common goal. The favors might be as simple as giving each other emergency provisions during snow storms, or they might expand into ongoing arrangements like sharing power tools or sitting for each other's pets. The exchange of favors provides the contact necessary to get to know one another. As that happens, you may find yourself talking about mutual concerns, like the vacant lot at the end of the block. Eventually, real friendship may blossom.

One mother who lived in a two-family house found that her work schedule made it impossssible for her to pick up her son at nursery school two days a week. She arranged for a baby-sitter to care for her child those two afternoons, but there was a half-hour gap between the end of school and when the sitter was available.

Searching for a solution, she timidly asked the sixty-three-year-old widow who lived in the other half of the house if she might be able to pick up the child at the school, which was a block away, and watch him until the sitter arrived. She knew her neighbor would be offended if she offered to pay her so, instead, she promised to run errands for her in return. The widow accepted the offer, and found that her weekday schedule had a new shape and structure. The arrangement eventually led to a strong friendship between the two women. The boy, who came to feel as though he had a surrogate grandma living next door, benefited from the sense of having an extended family. Meanwhile, the mother continued to "pay back" her neighbor by doing errands and other favors, and by surprising her with unexpected little gifts.

This notion of asking and returning favors brings us to the role suspicion plays in thwarting relationships. Many people are not open to the possibility of meeting or chatting with a stranger in the local grocery store, laundromat, or library because they fear they may accidentally get mixed up with a shady character or even a serial killer. They mistrust their own ability to judge character. Yet character need not be judged all at once. We can fight the fears stirred up by media stories of violence if we remember that there are many ways to be cordial in our dealings with strangers without throwing caution to the winds.

The world would be a considerably less lonely place if people were more inclined to greet each other in a friendly fashion and share some small talk. Such congeniality would also go far to improve the experience of standing in line for fifteen minutes, or waiting for the laundry to come out of the dryer. Oftentimes these simple, superficial conversations can make a lonely day less isolated, which in turn makes the world seem a less depressing place.

Still another way to make sure you have some social contact during an empty weekend is to plan your budget so that you can feel free to call friends and family long-distance. We know that many people can sustain their capacity for doing things alone if they have the opportunity to talk to someone who knows them well, even if that person lives on the opposite side of the country. Each of these calls should be treated as a time for refueling, fulfilling a need as vital as those satisfied by food and water.

It is important not to use these calls in order to vent the bitter feelings you harbor about being alone. Instead, make a purposeful effort to lavish on the person you are calling some of what you may need, be it attentive listening, sympathy, or curiosity about their activities. That way, they will enjoy the conversation too and feel inclined to give back generously.

The state of feeling single, lonely, and friendless is one that we have all experienced at some time. We have tried to map the road by which you can make your way toward having a circle of friends and activities that are gratifying. The trip may take longer than you thought but careful attention to the sites and landmarks along the way may prove more of a relief from loneliness than you expected. Further, the active process of sharing tasks and partaking in group activities may turn out to be satisfying in its own right.

# 8   Single Parenthood

The circumstances that lead to single parenthood are varied. Some of us are thrown into the role by the death of a spouse. Others come to it through divorce, either willingly or reluctantly. Some women become pregnant, purposefully or unintentionally, and choose to bear and raise their children without a father. A small but growing number of single women and sometimes men actively seek out the role by choosing to adopt.

Despite the different roads that lead to single parenthood and the variety of ways in which others react to single parents, those who share this status have certain experiences in common. Most obvious, there is no other adult living in the household to whom the single parent can turn for assistance, counsel, and companionship. To fulfill these needs, the single parent must rely on relationships outside of the home. Such relationships not only assuage loneliness and provide a bridge to the adult world, but they help meet practical needs, such as spontaneous child care when mom or dad is held up at work.

In general, the most overwhelming characteristic of single parenthood is the sense of being very much on your own. Many single parents are consumed by this feeling of total self-sufficiency, obscuring any vision of a rewarding, reassuring social life. Alone and tangled in a formidable web of responsibilities, these parents are often completely intimidated by the financial, emotional, and practical aspects of being the sole caretaker. As a result, they find it impossible to create the kind of relationships that would provide them with the support, companionship, and respite they so clearly need. It doesn't have to be this way. With courage and persistance, you can build a serviceable network of relationships which will help relieve the tremendous responsibility of solo parenting. At the same time you will enrich the lives of yourself and your children. The first step in establishing such a network is to develop confidence in your right to adult friendships.

All adults need adult company, just as children need time to play with their friends. Some single parents forgo the company of grown-ups, claiming that they are too busy or too overburdened to invest energy in adult friendships. Others feel guilty because their children are not growing up in a two-parent family. Mistakenly, they will pour all their energy and free time into paying attention to their kids. What these parents fail to understand is that when they isolate themselves from other adults, they do their children as well as themselves a great disservice.

Carol M. Anderson and Susan Stewart write in *Flying Solo: Single Women in Midlife,* "Parents in healthy two-parent families do not allow their children to consume their lives; they get their adult needs met in adult relationships—and so must single women. Without this sort of refueling, at least ocasionally, it gets increasingly difficult to manage the unrelenting tasks of child-care."[1]

If the single parent does not cultivate such social contacts, she does more than expose herself to loneliness. She also risks developing an increasing resentment toward her children. (We use the feminine here since the vast majority of single parents with custody of their children continue to be women, despite an increase in the number of men who assume this role.)

Observes Robert S. Weiss in his book, *Going It Alone,* "Without another adult in the household, failure to maintain linkages with friends and with kin produces a life barren of companionship, afflicted by boredom, without engagement, and without access to the help and information and support that friends and kin can supply."[2]

Developing and nourishing such linkages can be a formidable task. At the same time, becoming a single parent is an enormous transformation. It affects not only yourself and your children, but your friends and relatives. The new role involves so many changes that it is difficult to imagine that the single parent's other relationships would or could remain the same.

At twenty-six, Jamie knows that this is true. He had only been married a year when his son was born and his wife left. Within several months of becoming a parent, Jamie became a single parent. Five years later, he continues to care for his son, who has almost no contact with his mother. Jamie works during the day and goes to school at night and only dates when it doesn't interfere with his child's schedule.

As he explains, "I'm an old twenty-six. Most of the guys I grew up with are still single. I've left that life far behind, so I don't have many friends. Being a single father kind of isolates me."[3]

While Jamie's situation separates him from his former friends because they have yet to embark on marriage and parenthood, other single parents find that a gulf develops between themselves and their married friends. Particularly when single parenthood results from marital breakup, married friends are likely to perceive you differently.

As Robert Weiss notes, "The newly single woman may feel she is seen as a threat by both the wives and the husbands. The wives appear to her to be alert lest she attract the husbands' attention; the husbands appear a bit worried that she will inspire their wives to become more independent themselves."[4]

Other married friends may feel threatened by your new status because it stirs up uneasy feelings about difficulties they have been experiencing in their own marriage. They avoid you, almost as if divorce is contagious.

Weiss adds, "Only a minority among the widowed, and a still smaller proportion among the separated and divorced, continue to construct their social worlds from the friendships of their married lives. This is not to say that the friendships of married days are entirely lost; rather, they fade in importance. There is less sense of closeness in them, more sense of lives that have taken diverging paths."[5]

"To be single again is to end a way of life," observes Mildred Hope Witkin, Ph.D., in her book, *45 and Single Again.* "Sometimes it doesn't seem that way. Men and women seeking divorce, for example, may continue to do the same work, keep the same hours, engage in the same recreations, even see the same friends. Then one day they move from one bed to another bed, from a home shared for years to a home just starting to be created. That move, that shift, is a break in history, a cracking of the earth along a fault line; nothing will ever be the same again."[6]

Recognizing the enormity of the change and coming to terms with the way others react to your situation are two major aspects of the journey into single parenthood.

## Growth and Change

The journey we speak of begins with managing the transition to single parenthood and then continues on to the establishment of a new community of relationships. Many single parents have a hard time getting started, often because they fail to distinguish between what their kids need and what they want. These parents sacrifice their own needs to ease the guilt they feel for raising their children in what they view as a less than ideal family situation. Eventually they end up feeling angry and resentful.

Family psychologist and parenting columnist John Rosemond comments, "As a single mother, you must establish an identity for yourself separate and apart from the role of parent. You must allow the adult woman in you to separate herself from her role as Mom. Doing so will help you get your needs met, whether they be social, vocational, recreational, or sexual."[7] We think similar advice certainly applies to single fathers.

The key to creating a new, satisfying life is to view your new status as a single parent not as a defeat, but as the tinder that can spark the fires of personal growth. Yes, you may be lonely, and yes, loneliness can be painful and depleting, but keep in mind that many married people—particularly those who are unhappy in their relationship—also experience loneliness. As *Flying Solo* authors Carol M. Anderson and Susan Stewart observe:

> "Women can gain an enormous sense of mastery and self-esteem by surviving and even flourishing on their own. Taking control of their lives, loneliness and all, allows them to value themselves in unprecedented ways. Their comfort with time

alone is far greater than anyone immersed in the marriage and motherhood mandate, and the cultural myths it spawns, could predict. Those women still hanging on to the myth of the prince, those still caught in the web of waiting, may continue to experience loneliness as an acute problem."[8]

Women who are able to accept being alone as a natural part of life recognize that aloneness is not necessarily synonomous with loneliness. As one woman observed, "Do you look at it as loneliness or do you look at it as freedom?"[9]

Single parents who seize the opportunity to define new lives for themselves are often surprised at their own resources. As Carol, a social worker with two young sons observed, "The first Christmas after I got divorced was really hard. The kids were going to be far away with their father over school vacation, and I didn't know what I would do without them."

Carol initiated a whirlwind of preholiday family activities, including an all-day session baking edible Christmas cards, so that she wouldn't feel she had completely missed out on celebrating with her children. She also made sure to let her friends know that her children would be away and that she would love to be included in their festivities. She was invited to a Christmas Eve party, where, she says, "I missed my kids tremendously, but at the same time, I was grateful to be with people that I like instead of home by myself."

In the years that followed, Carol refined her system ("I found getting a few traditions established with the kids was good enough, that I didn't have to knock myself out") and came to peace with the fact that she would seldom celebrate the holiday itself with her children. "I never got over missing them," she says, "but I got to the point where I could really enjoy myself without them."

Other single parents, particularly men, are faced with the challenge of using their new status to catapult themselves beyond typical gender stereotypes. This is true particularly if their children are very young. The custodial father finds himself preoccupied with day-to-day routines of child care and managing a household. As *Going It Alone* author

Robert S. Weiss explains, the man who has recently become a single father may feel marginal in the company of couples. Weiss notes that "Some of his concerns—arranging children's activities, for example— are closer to those of the women in the group than to those of the men. But he can hardly enter into their discussions, a single man among women. With the men, he is conscious of how different his situation is from theirs, and again he feels marginal."[10]

The positive side of this situation is that many men who take on full-time single parenting discover parts of themselves they never knew existed. As they comfort and care for their children, they become more at ease with their own emotions and their own capacity to nurture. They use their single parent status as an opportunity to grow beyond typical gender stereotypes, and in doing so, they enhance their chances of developing new meaningful relationships in the years ahead.

Still other single parents have difficulty seeking out social contacts because, often without realizing it, they see themselves as defective. They identify themselves as damaged goods, as half of a couple rather than as an autonomous individual in their own right.

"Before my separation," says Stephen Atlas, author of *The Official Parents Without Partners Sourcebook*, "I viewed myself primarily in terms of my faults: being a mediocre handyman, not having a prestigious job, and frequently lacking the emotional energy to provide much understanding and support to my wife. When we separated, I had virtually blocked out any strengths that I had. When my friends invited me to join them on a weekend camping trip, my first reaction was fear: 'I haven't camped in years; I've forgotten what I knew. I'd be a burden to all of you!' One of my friends looked at me in amazement and replied, 'Hey, it doesn't matter to us if you're a good camper. If you want to learn to camp, we'll be glad to help you. If you just want to enjoy our company, that's all right, too.'"[11]

Those of us who become single parents when our children are in their teens and early twenties often face an additional challenge. Our offspring may distance themselves from us when they perceive that we are as needy and unable to cope as they are. When they were small, they counted on us to protect them from the world. They may be grown up or nearly so now, but the trauma of death or divorce can set them spinning and reignite the feelings and fears they experienced as children. When they see mom or dad fall apart, the foundations of their lives may tremble. If they cannot trust their parent to be strong and in control, whom can they count on?

While we desperately want the support and approval of these grown children as we adjust to our singleness and, eventually, begin perhaps to seek a new mate, we need to recognize that our children continue to see us as the parent. The best way to nourish relationships with grown children is to promote our own growth. When we take purposeful steps towards establishing a new identity as a single adult with a future, our children see us as competent and in control.

At the same time, we need to be careful not manipulate our children into taking our side or pitying us. When we take responsibility for ourselves, our children will see that while we are sometimes overwhelmed and lonely, we have not lost our strength and maturity. When we wallow in the past, we frequently repel our adult children. When we are able to acknowledge loneliness as a natural and appropriate part of our new status, we can begin to move forward. By taking responsibility for the quality of the years ahead, we enlist these same children to actively support our journey.

Learning to become comfortable with ourselves, frailties included, is very much a part of becoming a single parent. It is a process, however, which does not take place in a vacuum or in a set period of time. Ultimately, it goes hand in hand with building a new life secure in the role of single parent.

## Old Friends, New Friends

The challenge that faces single parents is to develop a community of friends and acquaintances that complements their new status. This community may well include couples that you socialized with in your married life. But you need to be open to the idea that the nature of old friendships may have to change. You may find, for example, that married friends no longer include you in their dinner parties. That kind of exclusion hurts, naturally, but instead of dwelling on your disappointment, try to focus on those parts of the relationship that continue to work. If you are inflexible, you may well find old friends quietly disappear.

We are reminded of Angela, whose husband died from cancer when she was just forty-two. A vivacious, affluent woman, Angela was used to weekends filled with social engagements, many of them involving her husband's business associates and their wives. These people were there for her during her husband's illness and immediately after his death, but they seemed to evaporate as the months went by. Angela was shocked to discover that she was no longer included in their gatherings. The women frequently invited her for lunch or to join them for a theater excursion, but Angela turned the invitations down cold. It was the beginning of a pattern that has continued for the past fifteen years.

"My mother never really had any friends after my father died," explains Angela's daughter, who is now a college student. "She was so resentful when she was asked to do things with a group of women, that she offended just about everyone who invited her anywhere. So, they just stopped asking. That meant she leaned on me all the time, wanting to go shopping with me and my friends, or out to lunch, and it got so I felt like I was suffocating."

Angela failed to rise to the challenge of establishing a new community of friends. Instead of making the most of the invitations to socialize that came her way, she became obsessed with resenting the ones that failed to materialize. In the process, she truncated relationships with old friends. Had she been able to acknowledge that those relationships were largely built around her husband's business, she might have been able to understand that it would take time for these friends to work out a different way of relating to her in her new role as a single parent.

Many new single people fail to recognize that they have one distinct advantage in reworking old friendships and forming new ones that they did not have when they were married. Think back to the time when you were half a couple. When you met new people at work or in the neighborhood, did you think about how your spouse would react to them before deciding whether to invite them to your home? Do you remember forgoing an afternoon with your women friends because you didn't want to leave your husband by himself? Those problems don't exist any more. The only person who needs to give you permission to pursue a friendship is yourself.

Part of the process of cultivating a new community of friends who are compatible with and supportive of your present situation is to open your arms to people whose circumstances are similar to yours. Some single parents avoid others like themselves, just like the lonely high school student who resists hanging out with an equally lonely classmate whom she really likes because she thinks then the other students will identify her as a loser. They don't want to be cast in what they consider a second-class role. Attitude is what counts here. If there's another single mother in your neighborhood, don't avoid her; befriend her. (Of course, this assumes that you basically like her.) Recognize that you can help each other out and rejoice in your friendship. Through such friendships, single parents can provide their children with a network of adults and children who can function similarly to an extended family. Indeed, in some instances groups of single parents and their collective children have set up housekeeping together, reducing expenses and increasing opportunities for support and companionship.

Single parent friends are particularly valuable because they have firsthand experience in many of the difficulties you may be encountering. They can help you puzzle out what to do on Father's Day when there is no father in the picture. They can help you figure out how to broach the subject of jockstraps with your maturing son who turns crimson and stomps off to his room the moment you mention the subject. Indeed, other single parents can also help us when our children are grown up by providing a place where we can reveal our worries and anguish without overburdening our kids.

While single parenthood is certainly replete with twenty-four-hour-a-day responsibility, there is a form of compensation involved here; being a single person is in some ways less restrictive than being married. When it's just you and your kids, you can be more spontaneous. Friends may also feel that they can be more informal with you than when they identified you as half a couple.

When Laurie and her husband divorced after nearly twenty years of marriage, she found herself latching on to the family of one of her ten-year-old's friends.

"These were people I'd hung out with at soccer games for years," she recalls. "Our children were good friends and played together a lot, but the most I'd done with Maggie, the mother, was to share a cup of coffee when I picked up Adam at her house or when she picked up her son at my house. But after I split up, she started asking me and Adam to stay for supper when I'd come to get him. I liked her and I liked her husband and kids too so I always jumped at the chance. I was lonely and bored and I think Adam felt the same way, being stuck alone with me every evening. Sometimes I thought I should have said 'Oh no, we can't,' but the truth was we could, because there wasn't anyone waiting for us at home, and we wanted to, so we did."

Laurie made a point of asking Maggie's family over for a cookout or other informal gathering every once in a while but, she says, their spur-of-the-moment invitations to join their family suppers certainly outdistanced hers. "They fed us a lot more than I fed them," she laughs.

Now that Laurie is living with a new man and her son is a teenager with a life of his own, she doesn't see these friends that often. "But Maggie and I still talk on the phone pretty frequently and sometimes we go walking together. I think of her as a really good friend and I always ask them to my New Year's party. I'll always be grateful to them for taking me in when I needed it and I'm sure we'll always stay friends even if we see less of each other."

As we have seen in earlier chapters, reciprocity is often the key to developing satisfying relationships. People join together to achieve a mutually beneficial end or, as in a marriage, they participate in an ongoing give and take that defines the way they raise their children and live their lives both within and outside the home. Reciprocity continues to be a vital ingredient as the single parent reworks old relationships and develops new ones to complement changed circumstances.

The ebb and flow of helping out needs to remain a two-way street if the single parent is to successfully alleviate the isolation and loneliness that are so frequently an unwelcome component of this new status. Without attention to reciprocity, it is easy to deplete our friends' store of support and empathy. Alone and exhausted by the challenges of taking full responsibility for our children, many of us react like sponges. Our appetite for sympathy, assistance, and companionship is seemingly insatiable.

We need to take care, however, to look beyond our own pain or loneliness; if we do not, we risk losing exactly the resources we most need to cultivate if we are to heal and move forward. Friends and family can give only so much before they begin to feel used and overburdened. The simplest way to keep that from happening is to make a conscious effort to give back. That doesn't mean, of course, keeping even. It does mean purposefully keeping alert for the times when you can be the one to lend a hand. It means being openly appreciative. It means never taking for granted those who reach out to us so generously in our darkest hours.

## Relatives

For those of us fortunate enough to live near relatives we like, extended family can often provide the assistance and comfort a newly single parent craves. In situations where single parent status results from divorce, it is important to remember that getting divorced doesn't have to mean divorcing ourselves from our in-laws. Grandparents, particularly, can continue to be a source of support. If we have forged close ties with our former spouse's siblings, these relationships can also continue. Often, however, filial loyalties mean that they are first interrupted by a dormant period. As time passes, acceptance develops, and a new and different normalcy begins to take form. The former brother or sister-in-law realizes that it is possible to maintain a relationship with you without betraying their own kin.

Marianne, in her early forties, has a lively household including her husband and four teenage daughters. When her sister-in-law, Ann, finally divorced her abusive husband, Marianne felt proud of her and offered to help out any way she could. With two young children, including a four-year-old boy who takes medication to control his hyperactivity, Ann was grateful for the offer. She started bringing her sons over to Marianne's house, leaving them there after school for an hour or two several times a week while she went shopping or did errands. Then she started coming back later and later, and usually ended up staying for supper.

"That was okay for awhile," Marianne observes. "There are a lot of us and I don't have any problem with a few extras around the dinner table. Problem was, Ann would spend the whole meal talking about her troubles. It was an endless monologue. She really felt sorry for herself, and with good reason too. But after a while it began to wear thin. My kids would avoid coming to dinner or make excuses and leave the table as soon as they could."

As the months went by, Ann started going out in the evening. Since finances were a problem, she would ask Marianne or one of her daughters to baby-sit. Her youngest demanded constant vigilance, and Marianne's children soon grew tired of watching him. When it reached the point where Ann said it would be easier to just leave her boys there overnight and pick them up the next day, Marianne finally admitted to herself that as much as she liked Ann and wanted to help make her difficult life a little easier, she didn't like the way her sister-in-law was treating her.

"Ann got selfish," she says. "She was so wrapped up in her own troubles that she wouldn't let anyone else get a word in edgewise. And she got into the habit of assuming that because I've got all these teenagers, someone would always be willing to baby-sit. I had to tell her it had gotten out of hand. She was very hurt. She doesn't come around much anymore and I'm sorry about that because I really like her. If she'd just showed a little interest in what my kids were up to or if she'd invited us over for dinner once in awhile, I don't think I'd feel this way. But she was so caught up in her own problems that she seemed to forget that other people have lives too."

By failing to replenish the good will that was lavished on her, Ann wore her relatives out. She took advantage of their generosity, perhaps unwittingly, and in the process she made her own life even lonelier by making it awkward to hang out at Marianne's, where she had felt welcome and accepted.

There is enormous value, of course, in nurturing relationships with your former relatives. Your children may not enjoy a traditional two-parent family but that doesn't mean they have to give up having aunts, uncles, and cousins. One of the keys to sustaining such relationships is to consciously avoid any negative mention of your former spouse. When you focus on the role these relatives play in your children's lives instead of on the link they represent between you and your former mate, you can begin to appreciate them and cultivate their company for the simple reason that they enrich your life and those of your children.

This means laying aside old grievances and setting your sights on the future rather than rehashing the past. It also means appreciating and respecting the support your relatives provide (even if it isn't as substantial as you might wish), never allowing yourself to treat their generosity as an entitlement.

## Lovers

For many single parents, looking to the future involves thinking about dating and the evolution of new sexual relationships. In ideal circumstances, you will give yourself a chance to learn to tolerate the loneliness of being a single parent before looking for a new partner. You will learn also the difference between being alone and being lonely and come to understand that loneliness is a natural part of life and that it cannot be banished simply by keeping a frantic social calendar.

As Dawn B. Sova, author of *Sex and the Single Mother,* explains, "It isn't unusual for a single mother to become involved in a sexual relationship in an attempt to gain sorely missed adult companionship. Loneliness, fear of the future, the desire for emotional closeness, and the need to be part of a couple again, if only in bed, lead women who have no desire for sex into sexual relationships. Sex becomes the currency that buys companionship and attention. Conducted in this way, a sexual relationship is demeaned, and so are the people involved."[12]

To Sova's list of nonsexual reasons for having sex, we would also add the importance of touch itself. There is something magically comforting about the sensation of skin to skin contact, the warmth of another's body. Touch banishes loneliness, at least in the moment, more powerfully than any other act. Its power is rooted in our most basic physiology; body contact with the mother helps an infant develop the capacity to regulate its own temperature and other physiological rhythms (as well as improving the infant's immune functions).[13] The soothing, organizing effect of touch is freely given to children but is ordinarily unavailable to adults without a sexual partner.

The abrupt loss of comforting touch is a major factor in the loneliness of adolescents, divorcing adults, and particularly the elderly, for whom, until recently, it was supposed to be unimportant. It is not surprising that single parents long to bring touching back into their lives.

While some single parents may enter into sexual relationships for the wrong reasons, others avoid them because they hold the mistaken belief that having a lover is somehow not good for their children. Certainly children are poorly served when mom or dad introduces a constant parade of dates and lets them sleep over indiscriminately, but such a scenario is a far cry from the establishment of a solid, loving relationship that develops over time. As we said earlier, adults need to live adult lives and having a responsible sexual relationship is natural.

"As uncomfortable as it may be for my children to acknowledge that I have sexual needs," writes novelist Joyce Maynard, a single mother of three, "it would be more damaging for them, in the end, to grow up believing that it's okay for a woman to lead a life totally devoid of physical intimacy and adult love. One of the most compelling reasons why I left my marriage two years ago was my growing sense that despite our devotion to our children, there was one large responsibility of parenthood my husband and I were failing to meet. We were not providing our children with the model of a close and intimate relationship between a man and a woman....I ended my marriage over the belief that the relationship between a man and a woman should be rich and vital, on all sorts of levels. To endure the grief and pain that accompany the ending of a marriage and then not set about finding the very thing you missed most would seem wasteful, irresponsible and foolish."[14]

There is no one right answer to the question of when to date and whom to date. "Some fathers feel in a double bind when it comes to dating. They believe they should date only single mothers, because only another custodial parent would understand the need to place their children first," comments Geoffrey L. Greif, author of *The Daddy Track and The Single Father.* "Yet that also means that both parents will have little free time to work on developing a relationship. The result for those fathers can be an increasing feeling of isolation or a series of relationships that never develop a deeper intimacy."[15]

Mark, thirty-three, who is raising two teenage sons, was hesitant to start dating. "I held back. I kept away from the singles bars. I wanted to be careful in the beginning not to just jump right back into a situation just because of need, physical or otherwise. I'm glad I was able to hold back. I needed to wait until I was ready. I never thought that I'd ever feel independent or confident or not lonely again. But somehow or other, I have reached that point and I'm not afraid to be alone anymore or to get married. You have to be able to get past the loneliness. Now I can be more confident in myself before getting involved and looking for those qualities in someone else. I'm not bitter. I'm okay."[16]

Negotiating single parenthood successfully takes time and perseverance. It involves reworking old relationships to fit new circumstances, and initiating new ones that complement our present situation. It means reinventing the role of parent so that we can meet our children's needs without neglecting our own. It means, too, recognizing that we can give as well as get support and assistance, and figuring out how to act on that knowledge. Let there be no doubt about it: Becoming a single parent is a difficult path to follow, but it is a journey that can lead to enormous personal growth and the vision of a happy future.

# 9 Marriage and Other Long-term Commitments

We assume that most couples will drift apart. "We just don't have anything in common anymore" is a standard explanation for divorce. Listeners will usually nod sadly and affirm our conviction that, even with the best of intentions, people's lives usually diverge along separate paths. The shock that previous generations felt at the announcement of a divorce has been replaced by a modern sense of wonder when a marriage actually lasts. Venerable wedding anniversaries are celebrations of beating the odds. The promise of lifelong union expressed in traditional marriage vows no longer reflects our real expectations about how adult relationships evolve.

A group of demographers made headlines several years ago by calculating that half of all new marriages will end in divorce. While other statisticians have questioned the assumptions behind that particular calculation, divorce rates today are unquestionably high, approximately twice what they were in the mid-1960s.[1] Even these statistics do not begin to reckon with an equally impressive increase in transient unions between unmarried individuals. Clearly, a fundamental shift has occurred in our ideas about the permanence of intimate ties.

New attitudes, however, should not automatically be condemned. After all, it is the result of individuals making choices about how they wish to live their lives, taking advantage of new freedoms and a greater range of opportunities. The expansion of career options for women has loosened the economic hold that marriage once had on wives. The potential ability to earn her own way allows a woman to ask questions about the viability of an unhappy marriage that would have been foolhardy to entertain in earlier times. (In reality, this sense of economic freedom may be exaggerated. Most women do not actually fare very well economically after a divorce.)

The sheer "ordinariness" of divorce also encourages men and women to ask previously unimaginable questions and, consequently, to imagine what the end of a marriage would be like for themselves. These daydreams further fuel the cycle, making divorce even more commonplace.

Modern life is filled with choices. There are so many opportunities to change direction, to chase down a new interest, to learn and grow over the course of an increasingly long life span. Why would we expect two people to choose to share their entire adult lives with each other? In fact, while the divorce rate has increased, the rate at which marriages are ended by the death of a spouse has fallen dramatically as our general health has improved. Some demographers estimate that, because of our increased longevity, the average length of time a married couple lives together has remained essentially the same over the last one hundred years despite the high divorce rate. Perhaps this is the best we can expect.

We, of course, don't believe that it is. We contend that the likelihood of a married couple embarking on divergent paths is highly dependent on the way we approach and arrange our lives. If we are determined to embrace the goal of sustaining common ground within a marriage or any other similarly committed intimate relationship, what steps can we take to make that happen? How can we tip the odds so that, over time, we will still say about a partner, "We still have so much in common."

Let's return to the story of Joseph, the forty-five-year-old executive we met in chapter 1 who was depressed about his daughter leaving home and afraid to burden his busy wife with his sadness.

Joseph felt his sense of connection to his wife slipping away. He felt pushed aside by his wife's involvement with her friends, the children, and her many other responsibilities. As his role at home seemed to diminish, his life at work, including his relationships with coworkers, became more compelling. He worked closely with a married woman named Anne, who was about his own age and similarly estranged from her spouse. Anne reacted to Joseph's occasional complaints about his wife with similar confessions about the way her marriage had fallen short of her hopes and desires.

As their conversations became more intimate, Joseph and Anne felt increasingly close to each other and distant from their spouses. They went from sharing confessional lunches to planning business trips together. When they found themselves alone in a foreign city, knowing only each other, the inevitable happened and, as Joseph put it, "she made clear that she would do anything I wanted to do." He found himself marveling at her lack of sexual inhibition and the intensity of their attachment, although they were careful not to complete intercourse in order to avoid being technically unfaithful to their spouses.

Joseph discussed his dilemma in therapy. He felt "stuck in a rut" with his wife while he and Anne had begun to travel down a new and exciting road together. As he felt greater attraction to Anne, his view of his wife also changed. The more negatively he perceived her, the more reasonable seemed their estrangement. At least, he thought, he did not have to feel guilty. His wife was hopelessly preoccupied with her worries about the children; she could never enjoy herself sexually; she never paid attention to him when he tried to talk to her about the things that mattered most to him. Joseph sought the psychological imprimatur of his therapist. Since he "needed" to be with Anne to feel "alive," he reasoned, wouldn't it be fine to continue planning trips and other times to be alone with her?

Joseph's story illustrates not only how relationships break down but also how closeness is created and how it can develop increasing vitality. Put most simply, Joseph began to share less with his wife and more with Anne. Soon he felt far away from his wife and very close to Anne. Joseph's story is typical because the act of sharing is exactly how we come to feel close to another person. We usually think of ourselves as wanting to share things with the people we feel close to, but we also feel close to the people with whom we share things.[2]

Closeness is a spatial metaphor that captures the emotional state that develops around the act of sharing. Just what we share encompasses a broad range of possibilities. It may be personal information, our feelings, a point of view, a mutual task or goal, a predicament. The list is endless. When we share physical space, however, many other sharings will inevitablely follow—as Joseph and Anne discovered.

Closeness between two people is usually either increasing or decreasing. It rarely remains constant. When we share something, we feel close, so we share more, so we feel closer. Or we may be moving in the other direction. When Joseph and Anne began to work together, to share tasks and goals that they both felt were important and compelling, they naturally began to share thoughts about the rest of their lives, including their complaints and hopes. And as they shared more, they felt even closer to each other. When we factor in Joseph's frustration with what he saw as his wife's unwillingness to allow him to participate in her life or to share his own private thoughts with her, the feeling of aliveness he experienced with Anne can be interpreted as more than just sexual excitement. Thus, his shift away from the faithfulness that he had previously cherished becomes less of a mystery.

Close working relationships between men and women have brought with them corresponding problems with maintaining boundaries in the workplace. Our advice to someone who is lonely and single (chapter 7) is to find a setting where you can share an activity, an interest, a sense of common striving with others. Unfortunately, this formula for creating the possibility of romance applies just as well to married people who are not supposed to be looking for romance.

Historically, societies that segregate the sexes by task and by place were in part responding to the way that closeness tends to extend itself into new areas of sharing. With no wish to return to that sort of rigid solution, we need to be aware and perhaps even a little vigilant about the very natural progression of closeness at work. We must also find ways to insure that the experience of shared tasks, shared purpose, and even shared time that is automatically a part of being "on-the-job" with somebody is also built into our marriages.

## Childrearing as a Shared Enterprise

Raising children is obviously the central joint venture in many marriages. Are some approaches to parenting more likely to unite a couple over time? When does parenting instead drive spouses apart? We first became curious about the effects of a shared task on marriages when we happened to be thinking about two seemingly unrelated problems at the same time. First, we recognized the great number of couples we saw in our psychiatric practices whose marriages were breaking down. Second, we began to think about the kind of child care arrangements we would make for our own young children.

As psychiatrists, we noticed that many couples encounter major marital problems while in their fifties. Individual partners often felt that they had come to inhabit a separate world from that of their spouse. These couples, like most of their generation, had lived their early marriage years according to a "traditional" model; that is, the wives stayed home when the children were young while the husbands worked extraordinarily hard as sole breadwinners, seeking security and success in their careers.

These women often felt "imprisoned" in the home. This clinical impression was consistent with the findings of a major study showing that women who stayed at home with young children without benefit of a close adult relationship often became depressed.[3] Paradoxically, many women reacted to their depression and isolation by becoming fiercely territorial and protective of their job as "child-rearing experts." In doing so, they covertly discouraged their husbands from becoming more active participants in bringing up the children. Meanwhile, the husbands threw themselves passionately into their work. It seems likely that the men also experienced some depression during this period because of the pressure to "make it" in their career without other outlets to boost their self-esteem. If they were not successful at work, they were simply no good.

Often husbands and wives did not recognize that dividing the marriage into two specialized domains launched them on separate life trajectories. Early on in their married lives they lost the sense that raising children was a mutual task, one that could bind them together over a lifetime. By the time the children were grown, the husband and wife had drifted irrevocably apart. Often, one of them had also drifted much closer to someone willing to share the part of life from which he or she felt excluded. As couples' therapists, we found ourselves trying to mitigate the painful aspects of divorce far more more often than helping a couple to mend an ailing relationship.

After repeatedly noticing this pattern, we began to wonder not only whether the "traditional model" of marriage and child-rearing was beneficial for couples and their children, a question many others have raised. We also thought that a specific difficulty might be the disappearance of the sense of a shared task in the marriage. After all, this "traditional model" was itself a change from earlier traditions, such as family farms and family businesses, in which the day-to-day separation of work and child-rearing functions was less rigid.

As previously noted, its worst, this new separation seems to have led to lonely, depressed mothers raising their children as if they were in fact alone. While the women protected their "turf," the men found ample support in the surrounding culture for focusing their energies exclusively on work. Then, after the children left home, the parents' marriage often fell apart, if it had not done so earlier. Of course, many couples were able to successfully share the task of child-rearing despite the pitfalls we have mentioned. But we were increasingly impressed by the obstacles to a sense of collaboration within a marriage.

It was at this point in our thinking that our own hypotheses became clearer. Is it possible, we wondered, that women who work part-time at something other than child-rearing during the early years of mother-hood, and therefore have an additional source of self-esteem, feel less depressed than those who devote themselves exclusively to taking care of their children? And might these women then be less territorial about child-rearing and allow, indeed demand, greater participation from their husbands?

We also speculated that this increased participation would renew the sense of child-rearing as a mutual task that could sustain a marriage over the decades. If evidence for these hypotheses could be obtained, it might prove to be of practical importance because it would underline the need to create more part-time jobs for women and, in the long run, for men as well.

We also hypothesized that, in all these respects, part-time work would be preferable to full-time work. Like full-time mothers, full-time working women invest most of their energy in one area rather than "diversifying" between children and work. And, unless husband and wife happened to work together, a shared task would still be missing in the marriage. Despite the financial advantages of a full-time dual career arrangement, the likelihood of diverging trajectories seemed as strong in this model as in the "traditional" one. The problem was further compounded by the additional burden of guilt working mothers feel when they are not the primary caretakers for their own children.

The existing literature offers many competing claims about the effect of work status on marriage, but the few studies that have focused specifically on part-time employment find surprisingly that such an arrangement increases marital satisfaction for both women and men. Our own pilot study of thirty couples with at least one child younger than five years of age examined differences between couples in which the wife worked full-time, part-time, or had no paid employment outside the home. Our results also support the idea that part-time employment for women increases a couple's shared involvement in child care and also increases their sense of sharing and connection with each other.[4] The number of couples in this preliminary study proved too small to provide statistical "proof" of the hypothesis, but much of the interview data was powerful and compelling.

All the couples interviewed felt that they were living through an intensely satisfying yet extraordinarily stressful time of life, characterized by the feeling of not having enough time to get everything done. As one mother put it, "Sometimes with our schedules, being a flesh and blood human being is tough." Another mother said, "It's really like you're on a roller coaster and you just have to hang on."

When women work part-time, however, their husbands spent more time involved with child care and both spouses were more likely to describe a greater sense of closeness, which grew out of their shared, if sometimes frenetic, activity. In their own words, both women and men in the part-time group give a sense of the quality of the bonds they established:

> "We obviously have less time to spend with one another and to have fun with one another. But I certainly feel that the magic is still there in the relationship. There is a closeness that wasn't there that was brought by having some kids in the house and the work that's involved in being together."

> "(Our life together since having children) is richer and realer, not euphoric but real."

> "I think we just have less time for one another (since having a child). But we're closer because of sharing and having Diana.... We're probably much more secure in our relationship with one another, but we have less time and probably less romance as it's defined in popular songs and stuff like that."

> "We are able to constructively help one another with the child rearing and without either one of us being the scapegoat, and so we've been able to help each other to grow in that respect. That brought us closer. It's as strong in terms of my feeling for her as it ever has been."

> "Well, we certainly have one more thing in common. There's more work to do so we end up sharing more work."

As an aside, we were interested to find that the husbands of women who worked part-time, not full-time, spent the most hours caring for their children. We suspect that the men in the part-time group were more involved with child care because their wives provide them with an appealing model of combining work and child care. When a wife works full-time, it is easier for both parents to justify leaving the child care in the hands of paid providers. In addition, since full-time childcare is already in place, the practical and interpersonal pressures on the husband for greater involvement in child care that exist in the part-time model are absent, just as they are with an at-home mother.

Only a study that follows couples over several decades can tell us whether these shared tasks actually decrease divorce rates. However, it seems clear that the couples who approached caring for their children as a joint endeavor experienced a particular combination of excitement and security in their relationship that seems likely to have "staying power." Couples in all categories described changes in their friendships, underlining how difficult it is to stay close to someone who does not share in your everyday concerns and activities. Almost all our subjects said that they had lost touch with old friends who had no children and that they had developed new friendships with other parents. For example:

> "We gravitated toward meeting other couples that have children because you form a little bit of a support network and that's one of the most helpful things that I have right now. On Saturdays I like to get the other mothers or fathers. We go to a swimming class in the morning and we all get together at someone's house and kind of coffee klatch and put the kids all together. It's pleasant and then we can all complain together and feel better."

> "You definitely relate a lot better to people who have children. It's just that there are a lot of things you have to talk about, or find out about people before you can really find out what makes them tick. When they have children close to yours in age, you don't have to go through all that because you know what they're going through—they're experiencing what you're experiencing. And also feeling that people without kids don't understand you—don't understand what you're doing day-to-day."

### A Brief Aside About the Children

While we have emphasized the ways in which a shared approach to child-rearing benefits parents, obviously the equally important question is how it affects children. A 1994 poll conducted in 1994 by Louis Harris and Associates points with surprising simplicity to the benefit that a basic act of sharing brings to children.[5] In a sample of 2,130 high school seniors, those students who said their "whole family sat around a table together for a meal" four or more times a week scored much higher on a test of academic achievement than other students. Even more striking is the fact that this effect was present in every subgroup that the pollsters analyzed: whites, blacks, Hispanics, students whose parents were college-educated and those whose parents never went to college.

The interpretation of this finding is complicated. A shared meal may simply reflect a family's overall style rather than producing any direct effect on academic performance. A part of the message is clear however. If family members cannot regularly shift their attention away from their separate concerns and responsibilities to focus on each other, the children are at a great disadvantage. The traditional ritual of sharing—breaking bread together—may serve as a simple marker of that commitment and attention.

### Sharing Without Children

Of course, not all couples have or want children and even those who do are not involved in raising them forever. Jim, one husband in our study, was already wondering about the next phase:

> "I love the things we do together. I love the age. I love the discoveries that we're going through but I don't know where to find the time for me.... So the whole issue of self-expression is beginning to emerge again. The kids are getting to a point were they don't need people all the time, and I think both of us are wondering what we're going to be doing."

Will Jim's search for self-expression inevitably lead him away from the shared adventure with his wife that he evokes so well? Will their next stage of growth mean that they grow apart? Again, the answer will depend in part on whether Jim and his wife continue to have mutual projects and goals that keep alive their sense of shared discovery. If not, their paths will start to diverge and any new discoveries that each of them make are likely to occur in the presence of others.

Some couples have jobs that, for better or worse, bind together their daily efforts and hopes, whether through the traditional American dream of starting a small family business or the more recent development of husband and wife sharing a common profession. In many ways these couples are lucky—the very process that lures unwary coworkers into affairs becomes a force supporting the vitality of the marriage. They can understand each other's experience with the immediacy and emotional resonance of an actual participant, not just a caring listener. They can choose to work together directly on a shared project rather than creating separate worlds in their work. Of course, this advantage comes with its own hazards for the marriage, particularly the dangers of competition and claustrophobia.

A famous portrayal of the joy and the complications of this type of marriage is found in the movie *Adam's Rib*, often described as a "classic comedy about the war of the sexes." Katherine Hepburn and Spencer Tracy play a defense lawyer and an assistant district attorney married to each other, loving and battling with each other. The movie portrays a couple whose sharing creates an intense closeness and also shows how common ground can quickly turn into a battleground.

Closer to home, both the child care study and this book represent a shared task within our own marriage. These shared tasks actually have brought us closer. They have also provoked some impressive fights between us. The intensity of the experience cuts both ways. Important conventions of civility and restraint temper the expression of our opinions in the workplace, but most of us do not carry these conventions into our homes. When we transform our jobs into shared marital tasks, some compromise between these two modes of expression is a good idea.

Most couples, however, do not have the luxury of experimenting with shared jobs and must build sharing into other aspects of their lives. A seemingly endless stream of articles in magazines, newspapers, and books offers couples suggestions about what they can do together to keep romance alive. A pre-Valentine's Day article in our local paper, desperate for a new angle on an old advice-column theme, suggested shared visits to poolrooms, shooting ranges, and the racetrack as creative possibilities. There is certainly no need for us to add our own suggestions to this already rich and peculiar stew. We will only note that physical touch plays a unique role in allaying feelings of loneliness within a marriage just as it does for singles (see chapter 8).

We must stress, however, that a program of the latest romantic-ideas-of-the-week is not enough for the long haul, even if they can help make a weekend more fun. Rather than building a world to live in side by side, a couple starts to feel like tourists who visit all the latest attractions together but soon become bored with their haphazard travels and with each other.

To deepen and sustain a relationship, interests must be shared over time and activities must involve mutual effort as well as mutual pleasure. Only then will a couple experience growth and change through what they share and feel actively involved in the creation of a common future. And only then will marriage itself offer the possibility of the ongoing transformation and discovery that are so often the dangerous bait of an extramarital affair.

Our friends Meg and John faced a particular challenge in their efforts to create a shared married life. They did not plan to have children together (John had grown children from an earlier marriage), but the absence of that potential bond also provided them with greater freedom to merge previously separate activities.

John's work as a freelance business consultant required a fair amount of travel and time away from home. Meg had worked in a business office, but her real interests and talents were in crafts and design, along with a sound knowledge of construction acquired from her father's work as a contractor. John's specialty was running work-shops in "team building" (more on that in the next chapter), so perhaps a professional respect for the importance of shared tasks added to his natural wish to be with Meg as much as possible.

Over several years, each became intimately involved in the other's most cherished enterprises. Meg took over the design of the manuals for John's training sessions and used her skill as a calligrapher to create certificates for the participants. Once she had a useful role to play, she became more comfortable accompanying John to some of his workshops, making them into shared expeditions rather than separations.

John and Meg also took on the renovation and later, the construction of a new home. Here Meg played the lead role, overseeing the contracting and design, with John as her enthusiastic collaborator. Their marriage thrived as they shared more of previously separate worlds.

## Too Much of a Good Thing

We do not want to overstate our case. Some joint projects are marital disasters. For awhile, we began to believe that any couple we knew who renovated a house together would end up divorced. Two caveats are in order. First, the shared task must genuinely reflect shared interests and goals. If someone feels roped into a project that really "belongs" to someone else, the shared task becomes a wedge rather than a bond. A spouse's enthusiasm can initially sweep their partner into a new interest, but the enthusiasm must be catching for the project to become "ours."

The second caution is that a marriage can also become endangered when a couple turns too far inward and loses its connections to the larger world. When couples in treatment complain that they no longer see other couples socially, we have been surprised to find that talk of separation is often just around the corner. When a couple lacks a larger social network to support and value them as a couple, they can easily feel claustrophobic, too dependent on each other. The pressure on each spouse to be all things to the other becomes too great, and it begins to generate resentment and irritability rather than greater closeness. The intense romance experienced by two lovers gazing only at each other can be the reason why two people marry, but it cannot be the only nourishment that the marriage receives.

There is yet another reason to worry about isolated couples. Just as child abuse is more likely to occur when social networks are severely limited (see chapter 3), spousal abuse or even simple unkindness is most likely to occur when the blinds are always drawn. A couple's moments alone together allow love to grow, but a married life lived in complete privacy can breed a kind of cruelty that is less likely to develop under the scrutiny of others. Such isolation can also beget intense loneliness. In healthy marriages, partners experience a deep level of sharing, but they also enjoy a web of subsidiary relationships, both as a couple and separately.

A friend of ours bridges the different parts of his life with an approach that is both innovative, yet harks back to older traditions in our country. Hal, a carpenter, is happily married and the father of a young son. For many years, he and several male friends would take a wilderness canoe trip in northern Maine for a week in the late fall. They all looked forward to the adventure and intensity of these days together, but they could not find a way to carry over their involvement with each other into their crowded everyday lives. Finally, they happened upon an idea that has become a tradition in its own right.

Like the proverbial shoemaker's children, their own families often went without the home repairs and improvements that these men provided for others. They began to take turns choosing a project that they would work on together over a few weekends for the benefit of both their families and their friendship.

The plan worked. Not only did they get things done, but their friendship seemed to move to a new level. It assumed a practical importance in their daily lives. It gave something back to their families rather than just taking them away for a week each year. And they discovered that their friendship was not "corrupted" by adding a shared self-interest to the purity of their time together in the northern woods. Instead, woven into the fabric of their ordinary lives, their bond grew more vigorous and sturdy.

# 10 Making Extended Families Work

Six members of a corporate personnel department hover over a table covered with LEGO blocks. Two of them start picking up the pieces, quickly fitting them together and taking them apart, then trying different combinations. Another pair talks animatedly, pointing to the blocks and using their hands to pantomime how they might position them. A woman stands alone, quietly sorting the pieces by shape. A man stands back, eyeing the blocks, seemingly lost in his own thoughts.

These people are participants in a workshop exercise session that focuses on "team building," a technique frequently used in corporate America. Typically, a company hires a consultant to take the key players in a particular department on a retreat where they will be free of the usual distractions. The participants are split into small groups and assigned a task, often an unlikely one such as building a structure with LEGO blocks or Tinker Toys. The consultant observes the small groups at work, noting individual and group work styles.

After a prescribed amount of time, the consultant might ask the participants to describe what they thought worked well and what didn't work within their group. The underlying theory is that people are more likely to notice their group style when working on an unfamiliar focused task than while immersed in their daily routines. They will then be able to apply this knowledge to the more amorphous tasks that are part of everyday work. The fact that the task is so different from their ordinary jobs is an advantage because it jolts the participants from their usual "ruts" and lets them see their interactions in a new light. Meanwhile, the very process of working together on a small project often leads workers to feel closer and more companionable.

How might this notion help families to function better? Most families have focused, task-oriented breaks in the routine of everyday life while preparing for major holidays and celebrations. Perhaps if family members took on diffferent roles than their usual ones during these preparations, and watched the way they interacted with one another, some of the lessons from the team-building approach might apply.

The hostess could become the guest, for example, and the clean-up crew could take up cooking instead. Families might discover that older members are tired of their leader positions while younger members appreciate the chance to try out leadership roles.

A careful look at how people function when they are asked to work together in new ways can have a salutory effect on families that feel they are calcified into ancient habits. It is not surprising that family therapists sometimes use this mutual task approach to create the possibility of change.

## Using the Shared Task

Far-flung extended families, in which relatives have little do with each other and can think of little to say when they do happen to cross paths, are commonplace in America. Even when parents live within an hour's drive of their adult children, which 60 percent of us do, a tremendous gulf can develop between them if they seldom or never do anything together or for one another.[1] We believe that grown children and their parents can use mutual projects and shared missions to breathe new life into their relationships just as consultants use joint team-building techniques to revitalize businesses.

When we say about someone that "he has the support of his extended family," we mean that something quite special and rare is happening—namely, that relatives outside the nuclear family are fulfilling a requirement essential to that person's sense of well-being. This kind of support can occur, for example, when a mother or mother-in-law takes care of her grandchildren while their parents go to work.

This arrangement is imbued with a wonderful evolutionary sim-plicity, except, of course, when the grandmother is unwillingly dragged away from her own chosen life. It can give the grandmother a renewed sense of purpose that she may have missed since her own children left home. At the same time, the son or daughter often feels more secure leaving grandma to care for the children rather than a hired baby-sitter who might tire of the job, because she has a vested interest in the children's safety and well-being.

Our neighbor, Mrs. Kilty, is a pillar of her town and church. When we first moved in, she and her lawyer husband set an example for the neighborhood of how an older couple ought to conduct themselves. If any of the neighbors were sick or pregnant, she would bring over a casserole at the time they most needed it. She gave neighborhood parties at which the food was splendid and her husband wore a velvet smoking jacket that bespoke an old-fashioned, opulent hospitality. And the Kilty's house and yard were always tidy, with bright flowers bordering the street. All in all, the couple seemed to symbolize how satisfying life could be for people in their sixties.

The Kilty's daughter, Joan, was an opera singer who had done well in her career. She was married to a supportive husband, Tom, who worked at a local radio station. Joan was pregnant with her first child eight years ago when her father suffered a heart attack. Although it seemed at first that Mr. Kilty was recovering, several months later he had a second attack and died. It was hard for people in the neighborhood to imagine Mrs. Kilty without her husband because they had been the proverbial "two peas in a pod." We wondered, what would she do with herself, and how would she ever get over the mourning process?

Because Joan had given birth to a healthy son just before her father's death, Mrs. Kilty had an immediate task before her. She needed to help her daughter, who had also been very close to her father. The urgency of caring for a new baby brought mother and daughter together during their time of mourning, although the shared task was bittersweet because Mr. Kilty could not be part of it.

It soon became clear that even though Joan's husband was a very devoted father, Joan's singing career could only continue if her mother accompanied her and the baby on trips to concert engagements in other cities. After a hiatus, Joan's music career began to flourish again, and Mrs. Kilty had a "raison d'etre." Soon their mom, pop, and grandma operation expanded. Joan began to give voice lessons at her mother's house because the location was more convenient for her students and it allowed her mother to care for the baby during the lessons. Once again, Mrs. Kilty's support made it possible for her daughter to continue her career.

Meanwhile, Mrs. Kilty's life was enriched by the knowledge that she was an essential, valued part of her daughter and grandchild's daily lives. She experienced a vitality that might well have been missing had she been limited to activities involving only people of her own age. Mrs. Kilty's story demonstrates the way in which being an essential part of another person's life is part of what keeps depression at bay. Almost every person who remains buoyant during the mid-life and elder years can point to someone to whom they feel vitally important.

But what is especially marvelous about the example of Mrs. Kilty and her daughter is that the give and take of their relationship enhances both their lives immeasurably. It is true that they had a good relationship to begin with, throughout Joan's childhood and teenage years. But without the child-care arrangement that brings them together several times a week their close relationship might have languished from lack of use rather than growing richer through the sharing of a new phase of life.

We are reminded here of Sue Bender's experience living with the Amish people described in her book, *Plain and Simple*.[2] She offers many examples of everyday customs that keep each generation in touch with the preceding one in a predictable way. One striking example is the "grossdadi house."

> As Lydia and I walked back along the path that joined her house to the small house in which her grandmother lived, she explained, "My grandmother and grandfather used to live in our big house, but now my parents run the farm, so they built a small house next door for the parents. It's our tradition—we switch houses when our parents get older. We call it the grossdadi house."[3]

Another excerpt from her book contrasts the Amish expectations about extended families with the norms of the authors' own neighborhood in Berkeley, California. Sue Bender writes:

> I knew the Amish refused to accept Social Security and medical benefits fearing they would become dependent on the outside community. How could Amos's family afford his staggering hospital bills [after he had an auto accident]? "Oh, the Amish Aid Society takes care of that. We take care of our own," Miriam told me.
>
> "How do you raise the money?"
>
> "We give as much as we can."
>
> These neighbors and friends had a kind of security that I didn't have. In times of sickness, accidents, financial setbacks, or natural disasters, they know support will be there. Miriam, who was seventy-eight and had sixty-three grandchildren, expected her children would want to take care of her as she got older, and it was hard for her to imagine that not happening.
>
> Brotherly love was their insurance.
>
> Who is richer, I wondered. How rich and varied my life was in some ways, and how poor and disconnected it was in others. "Let's pool our equipment," I had suggested to a friendly neighbor when I first moved into my home in Berkeley. She thought that was a great idea and for the next two years I borrowed her Electrolux vacuum and she borrowed nothing. The third year I bought my own Electrolux.[4]

Although we might not wish to return to a world as rigidly structured as that of the Amish, their society has avoided phenomena like granny-dumping, in which the elderly are dropped off at emergency rooms by relatives who disappear, never to return. Is there a middle ground between a society in which three generations live together regularly and one in which taking care of the older generation is severely neglected?

Once again, we feel that the answer lies in embracing the principles of give and take, in which different generations play active, supportive roles in each other's lives. This approach enables the generations to stay in touch so that we need never be left feeling abandoned during those phases of life in which we are naturally dependent on others.

In our practices we very often see older parents who feel frustrated because their adult children don't seem to want to use them as baby-sitters, financial helpers, or companions and advice-givers. Often they don't know whether their children are too proud to accept their help or whether they have somehow been so overbearing that their children will not risk letting them get too close. Meanwhile, we often see patients in their thirties who wonder why their parents don't volunteer to help more with their children, their finances, or their careers. Each generation seems entrapped by both pride and a lack of regular communication, which in turn make any discussion of these topics extremely delicate. Another patient provides an example of a parent who senses that she is drifting away from her children and yet cannot find a way to stop it.

Mrs. Anders is a fifty-nine-year-old divorced university dean whose children have finished college and moved away. An attractive, impeccably dressed black woman of Bermudan background, she has had to master the art of living alone. While she enjoys gardening, reading, and shopping for bargains, she feels ashamed of this last activity because it seems like a waste of time and money. Her own mother is spry at eighty-six and has a critical streak that leaves Mrs. Anders feeling emotionally distant. At the same time, Mrs. Anders worries that her own children feel similarly emotionally removed from her because of the critical tone that she recognizes in her own voice during her telephone conversations with them. Her son and daughter do not ask her advice and do not share their private lives with her.

Mrs. Anders comes to psychotherapy because she feels worried, sad, and lonely, although at the same time she treasures her solitude. Her pride prevents her from admitting to her children how unhappy she is about their increasing distance. Conversations in psychotherapy allow her to feel less angry and less hurt by them. Her empathy reemerges and leads her to approach them with more generous overtures. Soon her children are asking for her advice, as well as cooking holiday dinners with her in her kitchen. Mrs. Anders' loneliness decreases a little as she and her children become more involved in each other's lives.

### The Importance of Regular Contact

We are convinced that relationships between parents and adult children would often evolve positively and naturally if both generations could find a way to regularly give assistance to each other. Unfortunately, lack of regular contact can make even the most trivial interaction so highly charged that someone's feelings are likely to get hurt. Regular contact serves an important need even when it appears there is no specific reason for the encounter.

The situation is similar to dispensing with a committee meeting that appears to serve no useful function. It is not unusual to find that workers who used to get along well become mistrustful and paranoid about each other simply because regular contact is missing. This dynamic happens even more dramatically in families when young people leave home and try to conduct their relationship with their parents by long-distance telephone. An innocuous interaction that would have gone almost unnoticed when they lived under the same roof gets blown completely out of proportion during the phone call and each party is left feeling offended in their separate locales. When we see our relatives weekly, tempests are less likely to develop in teapots because the regular contact smooths out small rifts.

Mary Laveux, one of our patients, is a good example of a person who enjoyed a close connection with her family when she needed it most. She began psychotherapy at age seventy when she realized that there were difficulties in her marriage that would require her to change. Specifically, her husband, a prominent lawyer, had become very active in his professional organization. As a result, she was often left alone.

Mary wanted to use therapy to work at making a life of her own so she would feel less hurt by her husband's daily decisions to spend more time with his professional associates. Unfortunately, as she started to pursue some interests and friendships independently, he announced that he had fallen in love with a much younger colleague and was planning to move in with her. After forty-three years of marriage, Mary could scarcely believe this was happening to her. But the more she talked with him, the clearer his decision became.

As she moved through the next few surrealistic months of separation and divorce, she repeatedly remarked that being in touch with her four grown-up children saved her sanity. Two of her daughters lived in town, and one of them had two young daughters in preschool whom Mary took to school twice a week. The regular rhythm of seeing these two little girls, who were so full of life and who genuinely needed her, invariably brought Mary back from the brink of serious depression.

Meanwhile, her two daughters saw her every week and helped her with decisions, from the most mundane to the most complex. Her two sons, who lived out of town, were also very helpful. Not only did they validate her disbelief and rage that her husband could leave her at her age, but they also wanted to be actively involved with her during difficult transitions like separation, divorce, and selling her house.

Mary could become accustomed to asking for and giving help in a way that was contrary to her upbringing and to the habits she had practiced during most of her life. She only allowed this give and take to happen because she was in such dire straits after the divorce. In fact, her new willingness to give and take allowed her to develop her relationships with her children to a new level which culminated not only in the cooperative child-rearing of her grandchildren, but also in joint ownership of the family vacation house and shared summer vacations. The security gained from these solid relationships with her children allowed her to branch out and enter into friendships that she would never have risked while in her marriage. Gradually Mary came to believe that there was life after divorce, and that it just might be better.

A very different example is provided by Alison and Jerry, a strikingly attractive couple who married in their mid-thirties. This was Jerry's first marriage but Alison had previously been married to a man who died early on in their marriage. Alison, who was very young, was left to raise their daughter alone. She returned to her hometown to live near her parents, who helped her as she worked her way through business school. With much difficulty, and a great deal of financial support and child care from her family, she successfully raised her daughter, completed business school, and renewed her acquaintance with Jerry, a friend from her high school days. They fell in love and married.

Both Alison and Jerry held powerful jobs, Alison in a consulting firm, and Jerry as a deal broker in an investment house. After a few years of marriage they decided to try to have children, although Alison had mixed feelings after the ordeal of raising a youngster without a husband. Nevertheless, she felt she owed it to her husband to have a child. She had taken great joy in raising her daughter despite the difficulty of doing it as a single parent. Consequently, she thought her ambivalence might decrease in the face of a real baby.

The couple's efforts to have a baby proved unsuccessful and after a year of trying Alison, who was then forty-one, consulted her gynecologist about getting an infertility work-up. When it became clear that the work-up required various invasive procedures, Alison was unwilling to proceed. She and Jerry started working with a couples therapist to explore the question of how far to go trying to have a child and whether they should pursue adoption if pregnancy proved impossible.

As they explored this issue in depth in their couples' therapy, a new joint endeavor emerged in their every day life. They found themselves actively involved in raising their two-year-old niece, Laurie, who lived a block away with Jerry's brother and his wife. The day-to-day lives of the two families, in fact, were so intertwined that they would often congregate in one of their homes after work, helping out with child care and supper preparations while talking over their day together.

Alison and Jerry recognized that they had stumbled into a way to "borrow" a child without having to go the whole route of infertility work-ups and adoption. As a result they threw themselves into their support of Laurie even more wholeheartedly. Soon other members of Alison and Jerry's family were turning to them for support, not just in the realm of child care, but also for advice and good deeds of other sorts since they were such an effective team.

Alison and Jerry would become leaders in each of their families, a couple whom relatives could lean on. Jerry had played that role with friends and colleagues before they each started applying it to their own families. In their therapy they acknowledged that it was both incredibly gratifying in its own right and a reasonable substitute for having their own child. Becoming matriarchal and patriarchal in their own extended families was their new joint project.

## Family Owned Businesses

Family owned businesses offer another way that extended families stay connected together over decades. It can be a connection of great vitality, but also one of great pain. For every success, there seems to be a horror story in which family members have felt imprisoned by obligation to carry on a family company. American youth may sometimes feel overwhelmed by the number of career choices they face. In more traditional societies young people often felt constrained by the need to do what their mothers and fathers did before them. Some of them emigrated to the New World to escape that destiny.

Can we generalize about the pros and cons of a family business holding an extended family together? Probably not. Instead, we must appreciate that extended families, like nuclear families and individuals, are often in developmental flux. They have a life cycle of their own and a family can outgrow them. A family business for an immigrant extended family might be exactly what is needed to gain a foothold in America and employ other relatives who have just arrived. The all-embracing extended family that shares know-how, money, and decision-making has been a very successful formula for many new arrivals.

As the second and third generations come into being, however, a family business may outlive its usefulness, depending of course on the number and aspirations of the children. Usually the process of dissolving a family business is wrenching, since questions of loyalty and ambition are brought to the surface. Perhaps our mistake is to expect that developmental transitions of a family business would be any calmer than, say, the development of a family as an adolescent leaves home. In the latter case, we expect a great deal of turmoil as the teenager and his parents battle with complicated feelings about a child leaving the nest. Very often, a relative's departure from a family business is accompanied by equally powerful "sound and fury," as everyone grapples with the realization that things will not remain the same forever.

On a smaller scale, the idea of everyone contributing whatever they can to the family at large is illustrated by a family in which even an infirm great-grandmother has a role to play. One of us has a ninety-seven-year old grandmother, Mollie, who comes to visit Cambridge, Massachusetts, with her daughter and son-in-law several times a year. Although she has trouble getting up and down the stairs and her memory is failing, she can still cook Old Country recipes like borscht and noodle pudding. Her cooking projects need close supervision, but that too turns into an engaging shared task. The meals are well-loved and delicious, while at the same time, they allow Mollie to be useful in the day-to-day life of the family.

## Family Faiths, Family Causes

Finally, families can stay linked over several generations through their commitment to common practices, such as attending a house of worship together, participating in a political movement, or contributing to a common cause. We have found that if people are brought up with an active commitment in one of these areas, they usually have to find some way to weave it into their adult life in order to feel "grounded."

Thus, a child might be brought up to be a fervent Catholic by parents who took their religious affiliation very seriously. As a young adult, he might break with the Catholic religion over the Church's stance on abortion. If he never finds any new way to nourish his spiritual side, however, he is destined to feel a gnawing sense that things are not quite right. He may satisfy this need by becoming an active member of an Episcopalian church or even a Buddhist temple, as long as he doesn't ignore his spiritual needs entirely.

When several generations are able to practice at the same house of worship, the possibilities for generational interdependence multiply. The sense of being held within a common institution, sharing acquaintances and projects, is often particularly comfortable because the full responsibility for getting together does not rest on any individual's shoulders. The effect is similar when several generations of a family donate time or money to a joint cause or political party. For one family, the biannual fund-raiser of the Liver Foundation became a gathering that affirmed their sense of family unity because the life of one of them had been saved by a liver transplant.

A similar commitment to the care of a family member can also sustain the sense of a single family across the chasm of divorce:

Pedro, one of Dr. Olds's patients, was a twenty-year-old science student at a local university when she first met him. He was referred by the university health service because he suffered from intermittent panic episodes as well as seizure-like attacks for which the neurologists could find no organic cause. He was in danger of flunking his courses because his symptoms made it impossible to do homework or function in the dorm.

As he started therapy, he told Dr. Olds about his family in Mexico. His mother and his sister were extremely devoted to him, he said, and his father was a source of monetary support. His parents were divorced many years ago and there was still a very angry atmosphere between them.

Pedro became more depressed as it became clear that he could not manage his studies, and his therapist had to hospitalize him because of suicidal feelings. He dreaded an inevitable family visit to find out how he was doing. The worst, he explained, was that it seemed both parents were planning to visit and he could not stand the tension between them. He was also convinced that his father would be angry at him for letting this illness get the better of him. His father was very macho, he explained, and would not ever enter a hospital even though he had been dealing with depression for years.

His family arrived and as his psychiatrist, Dr. Olds planned a family meeting with great trepidation. She was especially worried since those participating had no common language. She spoke no Spanish, his parents knew no English, and Pedro would have to do the translating. The family meeting went amazingly well. Both parents were on their best behavior because they were so worried about their son and wanted to get the most help possible for him. Pedro told me later that he never would have believed they could function so well as parents. The most surprising news was that they continued to function well as parents for at least two years after this hospitalization, even though they were furious with one another on almost every other topic.

Later Pedro began interviewing for jobs just before he graduated. His mother and sister came to Cambridge to give him their full support. Specifically, his sister scheduled job interviews for Pedro, while his mother cooked, bought interview clothes, and gave moral support. His father was only available intermittently, but his financial support was invaluable and, for the first time, reliable.

When Dr. Olds reviewed Pedro's improvement, there was no doubt in her mind that his family had an enormously beneficial effect on him *and* that caring for him had brought out the best in his parents and sister. Their constant love and support had everything to do with his actually getting better and his need for help created a joint project that restored a sense of family to four disconnected individuals.

Generations are best able to stay in contact and deepen their relationships when they live in close proximity and share a mission or project. The most common example is a grandparent or grandparents taking care of the grandchildren on a regular basis. This mutually beneficial relationship often enhances the life of all three generations.

The next most common joint task is a family business, which brings everyone together with a sharp immediacy since everyone feels strongly about their livelihood. This joint endeavor is more likely to be a mixed blessing over the generations. Some family members may feel imprisoned by the joint task rather than choosing it freely when an independent career is seen by the family as a betrayal. Finally, a family value, such as supporting a particular charity, participating in a common religion or political party, or even taking care of a loved one, can knit families together in a common enterprise over many generations.

# 11 Networking in the Neighborhood

"Bloomfield Street's good neighbor"[1] trumpets a February 3, 1995, headline in the *Boston Globe*. The accompanying article describes seventy-two-year-old Stanley Galczynski and the kindness and favors he extends to his neighbors on the block-long stretch of Broomfield Street that makes up his Dorchester neighborhood. Galczynski and his wife Marianna have lived on the street for twenty-two years. During that time, the neighborhood has changed from predominately white to a diverse mix including African-Americans, Hispanics, and Asians.

Galczynski begins each morning with a 6:00 A.M. stroll to the corner store to buy a newspaper. He walks up and down the street several times a day, stopping to visit with neighbors. He might fix a gutter or a fence, or give a resident a ride to the store. "I watch out for my neighbors, all of them," he says. "I know what it means to help each other out. I bring encyclopedias to a neighbor. They are maybe old, but they are good and the neighbors are happy. They help me too. They shovel my walk."

It strikes us as a sign of the times that a major metropolitan newspaper would find such a story newsworthy. It was not so long ago that this kind of neighborliness was the norm. Now it is news. Reflecting the numerous social ills that beset our cities and towns, people no longer find it natural to connect with their neighbors. Often we do not even know who our neighbors are. This anonymity and insularity affects both city and suburb, and yet, there are neighborhoods like Mr. Galczynski's where people enrich the quality of their own lives by taking care of each other. As we have seen in previous chapters, participation in shared tasks often creates the glue that brings people together and serves to keep them from drifting apart. This is true once again in the context of the neighborhood.

When we think of the neighborhood and its role in alleviating loneliness, several factors come into play. High on the list are our own instinctive feelings about the kinds of relationships we would like to have with the people who live around us: do we want to be close friends with our neighbors or do we prefer to guard our privacy? Other important factors include the neighborhood geography—can one find playgrounds and parks, a corner store, a coffee shop?—and the availability of formal and informal groups, from Neighborhood Watch associations to garden clubs to people who swim laps at the local Y before heading off to work each morning. Let's take a look at the way these three factors affect a person's ability to connect with neighbors, share tasks with them, and eventually create a genuine and enduring sense of community.

## Cultivating Neighborliness

Renee Loth, a single woman, writes in the *Boston Globe Magazine* that she has moved into a new neighborhood where most residents own their homes and where almost everyone votes. She notes that her neighbors have not quite decided what to think of her. They seem to raise their eyebrows at her Question Authority bumper sticker and at the occasional male visitor who appears on her porch. But at the same time, they seem to approve of the work she has done on her house.

However, one thing sets her apart from others on her block. In a neighborhood of well tended hedges, her front yard hosts a rambling growth of unkempt hemlock. "My bushes," she writes, "get baleful looks from the neighbors, whose own topiary are trimmed at such sharp angles that you could slice a cabbage on them."

Loth leaves her hedge untended partly because she is wary of electric clippers and as a symbol of nonconformity.

As events would have it, she arrived home one summer evening to find her hedge perfectly manicured, courtesy of her neighbor. Instead of reacting with anger or indignation ("he shouldn't have done that without my permission!" Or, "it's none of his damn business!"), she responded with home-grown tomatoes and rosemary. Come winter, that same neighbor was out there clearing her a path with his snowblower. This time she rewarded him with cookies. "Luckily for me," she says, "sociability won out over skepticism and I have come to treasure the neighborly nosiness."[2]

We would add that Loth's own attitude had much to do with her success in connecting with her neighbors. Had she been self-righteous and angry, she might well have squelched the opportunity. Furthermore, by reciprocating with a gift, she further nourished the fledgling bond.

Many neighborhoods afford opportunities to develop rich relationships, but these opportunities are not delivered to the doorstep like the morning newspaper. We have to look for them, cultivate them, nourish them. Moreover, we need to be receptive, ready to fan a spark into a flame. Metaphorically speaking, however, the doorstep is not a bad place to start. Let's look at another example of how attitude—this time characterized by persistence—plays into the dynamics of forming neighborhood relationships.

Doris, a forty-seven-year-old black woman raised in New York City, moved to an affluent Massachusetts suburb in 1968 with her husband, who is white, and their new baby. At the time they were the only interracial family in town, which did not thrill the other residents. There were no overt expressions of hostility, but Doris could feel people avoiding eye contact wherever she went. She recalls, "If someone was weeding in their garden, when I went by they'd weed more intensively."

Doris grew up in a public housing project in the days when such projects were associated with low income and limited education, not with drugs and crime. In the warm weather, she played hopscotch and jumped rope in the concrete courtyard along with all the other kids, while their parents sat on the stoops, drinking beer, gossiping, and keeping an eye on their offspring. "That's where you met people," she says. "Outside, just hanging out on the stoop." Eager to make friends in her Massachusetts suburb, Doris decided to apply some of the socializing skills that she had learned growing up in the city.

"As soon as it got warm enough," she says, "I took the baby out for very long walks. I'd take the same route, every day, in the late afternoon, and I'd see the same people—stopping at the store for a newspaper, weeding, playing basketball, mowing their lawns, getting home from work. I'd say 'hello' to each one. Some ignored me, some would sort of nod, looking down. But I just kept following my route, smiling, greeting them, ignoring their silence. And then one day, a woman smiled back at me. The next day she said 'Hi,' and a week or two later she was looking in the stroller, trying to make my daughter laugh."

Doris kept accumulating the miles and by the time summer rolled around, she was on a first-name basis with half a dozen people on the block. One of them invited her family to a cookout. She brought fried chicken. From then on, it was easy. Within time, as they got to know her, not all but many of her neighbors became downright friendly. Her story shows that forging relationships takes perseverance. It also shows that a systematic approach can work. Taking the intitiative, making it happen, isn't easy but it certainly can be effective.

### Neighborhood Geography

As we have seen, persistence and the willingness to connect are two important qualities in the formation of satisfying social relationships. They are elements that can be either enhanced or stultified by the peculiarities of one's surroundings. If you feel anonymous in your own neighborhood, part of the problem may lie in the nature of the neighborhood itself. The physical attributes of a particular place can encourage or discourage sociability. In fact, the physical layout of a community is a major factor in the degree of isolation or connectedness experienced by residents.

"Land use is a mirror of society's social and economic values,"[3] observes Kate Warner, a professor in the Department of Urban Planning at the University of Michigan in Ann Arbor. Warner grew up in Mariemont, Ohio, a Cincinnati suburb designed in the 1920s. One of the country's earliest "planned communities," Mariemont's homes, businesses, and community facilities were grouped around a town center, all within walking distance of each other. Mariemont also incorporated a mix of housing options, ranging from single-family homes to row houses and apartment buildings, which in turn attracted a diverse population.

In contrast, many of today's towns and cities were designed with an emphasis on mobility. Instead of locating places to live, work, shop, learn, and pursue recreation near to one another, city planners separated these functions. The result is the contemporary suburb with its sprawling residential tracts and discrete shopping malls and office parks. In such communities, residents are often segregated into homogeneous residential enclaves, determined by factors like income, lifestyle, and ethnicity. As Ward explains, "We don't develop as communities, we develop as residential tracts, where you must drive from one driveway to the next."[4]

Many of these residential areas are built on the premise that the more separate and private the homes, the better. This value impedes the natural sociability that arises from regular encounters in mixed use neighborhoods, where stores, professional offices, restaurants, and recreational facilities exist within walking distance of the homes. Commenting on this tendency, architect Charles W. Moore observes, "As much attention is devoted to assuring privacy as money will allow, with no attention to providing for community, ever."[5]

In the quest for privacy we sacrifice small but vital institutions which have traditionally cemented us to our neighbors. We lose what sociologist Ray Oldenburg calls, in his book of the same name, "the great good place."[6] Great good places are those informal meeting places where people gather regularly to share news and opinions and to enjoy the pleasure of lively conversation on a regular, ongoing basis. They are the coffee shops, corner stores, and neighborhood bars. As we lose them, we sacrifice much of our vitality. Without the contacts they afford, we retreat into a series of homogeneous social encounters, diminishing the quality of our own lives and of our society as a whole.

The spread of the suburbs, where people must drive to get

anywhere, has obliterated many of these great good places. Increased mobility combined with the pressures of competing with well financed national chain operations has rendered many of the small establishments obsolete. Today the emphasis is on fast service and take-out. The old gathering places are disappearing, victims of a changed economy and changed housing patterns.

As Oldenburg observes, "The proportion of beer and spirits consumed in public places has declined from about 90 percent of the total in the late 1940s to about 30 percent today."[7] People are doing a greater share of their drinking at home instead of in neighborhood taverns. At home they do not meet their neighbors. The same is true of ice cream. For example, neighborhood soda fountains have fallen victim to impersonal chain stores.

The loss is not just that we do not drink and eat together. We have sacrificed public opportunities to connect. To remain vital, both cities and suburbs require public settings where people gather on equal terms. As Oldenburg writes in *The Great Good Place*, "If there is no neutral ground in the neighborhoods where people live, association outside the home will be impoverished. Many, perhaps most, neighbors will never meet, to say nothing of associate, for there is no place for them to do so."[8]

Without these public or great good places, our lives are divided between home and work. When realtors sell homes, they boast of spacious lawns, fine schools, and proximity to the seaside. They do not think to list the neighborhood lunch counter. Perhaps they should, because such institutions serve as indicators of the neighborhood's sense of identity. It is extremely difficult to get to know the neighbors if there is no place to easily and regularly encounter one another.

In cataloging the opportunities to form relationships in your own neighborhood, it makes sense not to overlook seemingly insignificant opportunities. Over time, small changes in your own habits can reap big rewards. Can you pick up milk in the evening from a small store instead of stopping at the supermarket on your way home from work? Rather than grabbing coffee at a fast food drive-in, can you go to a coffee shop? While such institutions are diminishing in number, they do still exist. Their role needs to be acknowledged and exploited. As you become a regular customer, you will find opportunities for conversation, perhaps with a much broader assortment of people than you encounter at work.

## Living Arrangements

When it comes to choosing the place you call home, there are choices to make not only in regard to the external geography of the neighborhood but in terms of your living arrangement. Typically, people have chosen to live alone, with a roommate (or more), or in a separate home or unit with their children and/or spouse. But other forms of residence have begun to evolve.

In recent years economic hardships have fostered an increase in the numbers of families in which at least three generations share one roof. For example, even though the number of individuals living alone continues to rise, census data for a cluster of thirty-seven contiguous Massachusetts cities and towns indicates that the number of families with more than two generations living together rose from 3,659 to 5,971 between 1980 and 1990, an increase of 63.2 percent.[9]

A combination of harsh economic circumstances and the changing structure of the American family have motivated an increasing number of people to participate in such a shared household. Many of these households consist of a single mother or father raising at least one child. Women with little experience in the work force are less likely than their male counterparts to be able to pay rent or a mortgage following a divorce, and have few options other than to return to their parents' home. In other instances, married adults return to live with their parents so that they can save money to buy a home of their own.

Those who participate in multigenerational living arrangements frequently complain of the loss of privacy and personal autonomy. One single mother who shares a mobile home with her toddler and her own mother, the child's grandparent, complains, "My mother always reminds me that I'm living under her roof and I have to do what she says. My mother is in control, but this is the only avenue I have."[10]

For other families, however, such an arrangement works out well. A Winthrop, Massachusetts, family with nine members representing four generations provides an illustration of the rewards of intergenerational living. Like others, the Mahoneys were motivated by financial considerations. "We were all living in apartments and knew we wouldn't be able to own our own homes so we got the down payment together and moved in together," explains Dawn Mahoney, a member of the grandparent generation.[11] Now the family divides the mortgage four ways and pays less than the sum of the rents they used to pay.

The household consists of John Mahoney and his wife Dorothy, their daughters Dawn and Denise, Dawn's daughter Desiree and her husband and their year-old daughter, Denise's twenty-one-year-old son James, and a family friend, Betsy. "We have hassles with each other every now and then, but we respect each, get along, and we have enough space," observes Dawn Mahoney, adding that "we like each other's company so it's a nice family environment."

"We're never hurting for company around here," sums up John Mahoney, the family patriarch.[12]

Shared housing is an old concept that has begun to take on new shapes. Motivated by economic concerns as well as a hunger for companionship, groups of unrelated people come together under one roof in a variety of circumstances. Single parents, for example, cite the support and assistance available to them when they live with others, particularly if the household includes another parent-child team with similar circumstances.

Shared housing is an option that can prove fruitful for single men and women, for single parent families, and for mixed groups of people too (some single, some married, some with children). In shared housing, the participants usually eat together and share chores. Mothers may take care of each other's children.

Felice Merton began renting out rooms in the mid-1960s after her husband died and her children had grown up and moved away. She usually had two boarders at a time, most often young people who worked at the school where she taught. Some stayed a year or two while others remained much longer. She charged modest rents and encouraged them to use the kitchen, the washing machine, and the garden. Most became friends. They went to concerts and movies with her, and as she got older and her eyesight failed, they drove her places at night. By offering them privacy and treating them as friends instead of tenants, she initiated a give and take that benefited her and them too.

Shared housing demands cooperation, tolerance, and flexibility. It offers companionship, the security of having others in the building, and, usually, a beneficial financial situation. For many, however, the togetherness of shared housing is overwhelming. Cohousing offers a compromise: separate living quarters with built-in daily opportunities to socialize with the neighbors.

In recent years determined individuals have begun to fight back against suburban sprawl and faceless cities that empty out each day at 5:00 P.M. Determined to live in neighborhoods that enhance their sense of interdependence, members of the cohousing movement purposefully design communities which encourage interaction between individuals. In their 1994 book, *Cohousing: A Contemporary Approach to Housing Ourselves*, (Ten Speed Press), Kathryn McCamant and Charles Durrett comment that traditional forms of housing no longer provide the sense of community, of belonging, that many of us used to take for granted. They point out that 67 percent of American housing stock takes the form of the single-family detached home, designed to accommodate a nuclear family of stay-at-home mom, breadwinner dad, and two to four children. With the enormous increase in the number of single parent families and the number of families in which both parents work, combined with the fact that nearly one-quarter of our population lives alone, this form of housing is no longer in synch with reality.

Cohousing communities combine "the autonomy of private dwellings with the advantages of community living."[13] Typically a cohousing community will be composed of fifteen to thirty-three households, each of which has its own private, self-sufficient residential unit. The community also includes extensive common facilities such as a kitchen and dining hall capable of accommodating all of the community's residents, children's playrooms, laundry facilities, and garden space.

Cohousing meshes autonomy with community. Each family determines for itself how much or how little it wants to be involved in community activities. Some people enjoy their dinners in the communal dining room nearly every evening, while others may join in only occasionally. Cohousing developments do not target a specific age or family type. Instead, they welcome a broad cross section of residents, which often makes them resemble a huge extended family. The communal dinners mean that working parents can relax with their children after work instead of rushing off to the grocery store and preparing supper.

For singles, the cohousing developments offer a sense of personal security missing in apartment buildings and single-family homes. For the elderly, they provide the stimulation of intergenerational contacts. For children, they present a rich reservoir of playmates. These are places, says architect Charles W. Moore, "where people have chosen to provide for community as well as privacy, where adults and children value each other, and remain interested in concerns beyond themselves."[14]

The cohousing movement began in Denmark in the early 1970s and is now well established in other European countries. In the past decade, hundreds of cohousing groups have formed in the United States and Canada. The movement is dedicated to reviving many of the attributes of traditional villages which are complementary to the demands and the realities of contemporary life. If you feel strongly enough about having a hand in shaping a neighborhood that supports your values and lifestyle, a cohousing situation could be the right match. By working together with a group to develop a cohousing community, you enhance the potential to create enduring friendships with people who may be your neighbors for many, many years.

Many of us, however, have neither the opportunity nor the inclination to make a radical change in our living situation. But that doesn't mean we can't enjoy some of the rewards delivered by the cohousing movement. It simply means we have to commit ourselves to exploring new ways of meeting old needs, with an eye to increasing regular interactions with our neighbors.

When our son was young we hired a young mother to care for him twenty-five hours a week. Heidi brought along her own child and so our sons were raised together. She often sat out on the front steps while the children played, getting to know other mothers on the block. She had her second child when we had our second, both daughters, and she then took care of all four children. Although she lived in a neighboring community, Heidi became an integral part of our neighborhood. She walked our children to nursery school and got to know the parents of their friends, and they liked her so much that eventually she was hired as a teacher at the school.

Because we shared an easy give and take, our arrangement proved particularly rewarding even though Heidi worked for us. Sometimes she and her husband would take our children overnight and sometimes we would take theirs. When she finally left, we decided not to hire anyone else. We had discovered how gratifying it is to simply trade child care chores with other parents. For the most part, we found that we could juggle our schedules to take care of the children ourselves, with a little help from their friends' parents.

School vacation periods, however, presented a problem. To fill this vacuum, we joined together with several nearby families to form a "neighborhood camp," which bridged the child care gap during school holidays and other difficult to cover times like the week before school starts. Collectively, we hired two teenage girls to care for about eight children. They alternated houses so the group got to play in a different place each day.

We were intrigued to see that children in the neighborhood who didn't need child care clamored to join just because they saw how much fun these youngsters were having together. Mothers who didn't work loved it because they could get some free time and the mothers of the teenagers loved it because their daughters spent vacations right in the neighborhood. The children who attended thought it was great because every morning they had a ready-made gang of kids to play with. As well as providing an important service to the parents, the camp enabled children who lived in the same neighborhood but attended several different schools to maintain and nourish their neighborhood friendships.

Our neighborhood camp proved a great success partly because we were fortunate enough to live in a community with other families who had similar needs. As we have shown earlier, some settings are more conducive to making friends than others. One important factor is the mix of people. While making a residential move is a big decision, and while there is certainly no guarantee that a change of residence will improve the quality of social contacts, there are times when a move is either necessary (e.g., a job change, a decision to live nearer family) or simply possible.

### Assessing the Social Fabric of a Neighborhood

When considering a new neighborhood, it makes sense to carefully explore the options, not just in terms of location and the type of home, but with regard for the feel of the neighborhood itself. Take long walks at different times of the day. Get a sense for the street life of the neighborhood as people go off to work in the morning, after school, on a Saturday night. Look for the kinds of public spaces that encourage neighborliness: parks and playgrounds, benches on the sidewalks, churches, schools. Figure out how many types of errands you will be able to accomplish on foot. Visit the nearest library and supermarket. Look for great good places, like small stores and coffee shops, and visit them.

To get a sense of the kinds of lives people in the neighborhood lead, check out announcements tacked to walls or bulletin boards. Are people seeking baby-sitters, volunteers to assist in a local political cause, or neighbors to join a book group? Scan the local newspaper too, paying particular attention to features listing community events and volunteer opportunities. Ask yourself, "What is it about this neighborhood that would make it a good place to form relationships? What factors might make socializing difficult?"

### Joining Organized Groups

Organized groups make up the third factor in developing community ties. The most obvious way to develop relationships with neighbors is to join the organizations to which they belong. Apparently there are no limits to the groups and causes one can join in most American suburbs and cities. Read the listings in almost any community newspaper and you discover that a variety of activities are available nearly every day and evening.

Certainly it is important to choose groups that offer an activity or focus that appeals to you. Yet it is also useful to evaluate the potential group or activity specifically in terms of its long-term potential. When it comes to forming enduring, genuine bonds, all groups are not created equal.

As former White House advisor Amitai Etzioni, a founder of the Communitarian movement, observes in his book, *The Spirit of Community*:

> "The best social events do not merely develop bonds, but also serve a Communitarian purpose, from organizing neighborhood crime watches to running soup kitchens. Groups that focus directly on the social relations themselves, like parties for singles aimed at fishing for dates, are often less socially constructive; more effective groups are those where members focus on bettering others and allow social networks to evolve as a by-product."[15]

Despite the obvious benefits, many of us avoid civic involvement. Robert D. Putnam, whose work we mentioned earlier, is the director of the Center for International Affairs at Harvard University. He notes that between 1973 and 1993, the number of Americans who attended a public meeting on town or school affairs in the past year dropped by more than a third. While the number of Americans belonging to church-related groups has declined modestly, membership in organizations like the PTA and the League of Women Voters has decreased drastically over the past generation. So has the number of volunteers who contribute to civic organizations like the Boy Scouts and the Red Cross.

A similar trend is also evident when it comes to a recreational pursuit—bowling. Putnam reports that the number of Americans who go bowling today is higher than it has ever been before. Between 1980 and 1993 the total number of bowlers in the country went up 10 percent, but during the same time period, the number of people participating in league bowling decreased 40 percent. We are bowling more, but doing it on our own. While bowling may seem an odd measure of our connectedness, Putnam makes a case for its significance by noting that "80 million Americans went bowling at least once during 1993, nearly a third more than voted in the 1994 congressional elections and roughly the same number as claim to attend church regularly."[16]

Extending Etzioni's premise that there is enormous qualitative difference in the ways in which people participate in groups, Putnam observes that while membership is down in traditional types of organization, it has soared in new organizations that reflect contemporary concerns. Environmental groups like the Sierra Club and feminist organizations like the National Organization for Women grew rapidly in the 1970s and 1980s.

They boast hundreds of thousands of dues paying members. But they do not represent an increase in the kind of social connectedness we have been discussing. Most members never meet another member and never attend meetings. They "belong" by virtue of writing a check, but this act in itself does little to encourage sociable encounters. As Putnam puts it, "Their ties...are to common symbols, common leaders, and perhaps common ideals, but not to one another."[17]

Findings from the General Social Survey (GSS), a national-sample survey conducted fourteen times over the past twenty years, further our understanding about the level at which most Americans participate in both informal and formal groups.

One of the questions included in this survey asks, "How often do you spend a social evening with a neighbor?" If you seldom socialize with your neighbors, you are typical of most Americans. The number of Americans who indicate that they socialize with their neighbors more than once a year has steadily declined from 72 percent in 1974 to 61 percent in 1993.[18] That means that 39 percent of us spend one evening or less per year with a neighbor. Sociable neighborhood relations don't just happen. As we stated earlier, they grow out of a combination of attitude, the physical nature of the setting, and degree of involvement in informal and formal groups.

The aggregate results of the General Social Survey indicate that the most common type of formal groups Americans join are church-related, particularly for women. The survey also gives evidence of a modest decline in church group membership over the past twenty years, from about 48 percent in the 1950s to about 41 percent in the 1970s, with little change thereafter.[19]

In our practice, we regularly encounter patients who struggle with questions regarding the role of religious institutions in their own lives. Typically, these patients grew up attending church or synagogue, and drifted away in their high school or college years. As they began to have children of their own, their thoughts turned to the role of organized religion in their own families. Some feel that it is important to have a spiritual affiliation, if not for themselves then for their youngsters.

Some are motivated by nostalgia; they crave the sense of belonging and togetherness they associate with their childhood years at church or temple. Others are conflicted; they want to make religion a part of their lives but they harbor feelings of resentment or frustration toward the type of institution they attended as children. Still others are clear in their own minds that they seek a place of worship because of the respectability and oppportunities for social connections membership implies.

Joining a religious congregation affords the opportunity to forge new relationships in a safe, predictable environment. Because much religious activity is built upon the assumption of weekly attendance, membership implies regular contact over a prolonged period of time, a major factor in the establishment of friendships. Because many religious institutions undertake good works, membership also implies the opportunity to engage with others in a joint task which benefits the greater community.

Religious bodies welcome the single, the widowed, the married, the young and the old. Their activities usually reflect the nature of the congregation. For some of us, joining a religious institution can satisfy both our spiritual and social needs. It is one more option to consider as you seek to strengthen and enlarge your own social network.

But remember always that joining a religious institution or any other organization simply for the social dividend seldom proves to be a a fruitful path. Unless you are committed to the broader mission of the organization, you are likely to find the relationships you form within it as tenuous as your belief in the ideals the group represents.

The act of joining is in itself only a beginning in the quest to forge deep and abiding human connections. The energy and commitment that one contributes after signing on ultimately determine whether such connections will evolve.

For those who are not comfortable with organized religion, involvement in local government offers a different kind of opportunity to contribute to the greater good while enjoying the opportunity to develop a diverse set of acquaintances in the context of a ready-made task. In Harriet Webster's community, for example, in addition to an elected school board and city council, there are more than two dozen appointed municipal boards and commissions, from the board of health and the human services commission to the capital improvements board and the public plantings committee. While competition is heated for some of the positions, a slot exists somewhere for just about anyone who wants to serve. Openings are advertised in the local newspaper.

Many communities also have active neighborhood associations, with membership open to all. Their activities reflect the members' perception of the neighborhood's needs. Like the formal government boards and commissions, such organizations offer the opportunity to participate in group problem-solving. Consistent with Etzioni's thinking, they afford valuable opportunities to form and deepen relationships because their focus is beyond the individual. Their efforts center on projects that benefit the community.

For example, in many parts of the country residents have organized Neighborhood Watch, a program designed to encourage neighbors to take responsibility for keeping their neighborhood safe. Working with the local police, they agree to a set of guidelines and procedures designed to keep tabs on any suspicious activity in the neighborhood. In some communities, neighbors form "safe house" networks, where parents agree to open their home without question to any child who feels unsafe walking to or from school or simply playing outside. Participation in such programs allows personal relationships to develop as a by-product of a shared interest—protecting each other from harm. This focus on a goal that benefits the community eliminates the tension and self-consciousness that can occur when one joins a group purely with the goal of making new friends.

For parents, involvement in school-related activities offers a natural path to new relationships. Schools often serve as neighborhood or community focal points. They seek volunteers as well as supporters who will lobby for their needs. Mothers and fathers who offer to help out—whether by joining the PTA, lending a hand in the classroom, or assuming responsibility for any of the dozens of other jobs filled by school volunteers, put themselves in the position of meeting other parents with children of similar ages. Developing relationships often happens quite naturally in this milieu because much of the conversation centers on a shared experience—being the parents of school-age children.

Traditionally women have done most of the school volunteer work, but that has changed significantly in recent years. With the proliferation of varied family structures, school groups have become ideal gathering places for mothers and fathers, couples and single parents. Participants are bound together by their interest in the education of their children.

Joining a group is a solid step in making one's place in the neighborhood and thus alleviating loneliness and isolation. By joining, you express an interest in the goal of the group, be it discussing books, creating a safer neighborhood, or improving the local school. At the same time you get to know people who share your interests. As mentioned in the earlier chapter on singleness, however, it is unrealistic to expect a quick fix. Joining a group is a beginning, not an end in itself. It takes time for relationships to develop, and sticking it out is a big part of the battle.

Research indicates that men are far less likely than women to seek help when overwhelmed with loneliness. For example, only 10 percent of those who belong to the American Association of Retired Persons' Widowed Person Service are men. "Women talk, men do," observes AARP spokesperson Judy Fink.[20]

Howard Thorsheim and Bruce Roberts, psychology professors at St. Olaf's College in Northfield, Minnesota, study the role of groups in alleviating loneliness and other problems. They discovered the ultimate male support group on a trip to Norway. Several retired whalers joined forces to buy a boat to repair. They admitted that what they really wanted to do was just talk companionably with one other, but unlike women, they felt they needed to be working on a project while they talked.[21] Their joint task gave them a context in which socializing felt comfortable.

As cohousing proponents McCamant and Durrett note, "A home is more than a roof over one's head or a financial investment. It can provide a sense of security and comfort, or elicit feelings of frustration, loneliness or fear. The home environment affects a person's confidence, relationships with others, and personal satisfaction."[22]

We think that their comments apply just as aptly to a neighborhood. A good neighborhood is more than a good school, safe streets, and well kept homes. It embodies a feeling of cohesiveness, a sense that those of us who live there are interested in one another's mutual well-being. Furthermore, we are willing and eager to invest our time and energy in getting to know one another and in taking care of our community.

Such neighborhoods exist in urban centers, suburbs, and rural towns. Sometimes they take the form of an apartment building, other times they embrace a single block or a series of streets. Whatever their shape, they provide a base from which to cultivate enduring, satisfying friendships.

# Part 4

# Putting It All Together

# 12 Conclusions and Cautions

A full life free from loneliness is almost unimaginable. It would have to be a life in which no one that we cared about was ever lost or absent. Either that, or an existence in which no one was cared about at all. Loneliness is an essential human emotion, not the villain in our drama. Loneliness functions like an alarm bell. It signals that something is wrong and calls for our attention. Its discomfort motivates us to change a bad situation, much as physical pain does. Like pain, loneliness becomes a problem in its own right only when we have no way to relieve it. Then it is transformed from a useful warning to a chronic disability.

The goal of this book is not to eradicate loneliness. To do so, we would first have to eliminate love and caring, or to change human nature. Robert Weiss, who has studied loneliness in divorce, single parenting, and bereavement, observes:

> "[L]oneliness seems to occur regularly when emotional life is unshared. Loneliness appears to be a quite normal signal of an emotionally unsatisfactory state, the state of being without emotional partnerships. Why humans should be so constituted is unclear, but it might be surmised that in the evolution of the human organism, loneliness proved a guarantor, desirable from the standpoint of progeny, that parents would remain bonded to each other."[1]

We would extend this argument by suggesting that loneliness also acts to protect our bonds with larger social groups, connections which have been just as important to human survival and development as parental bonds. Charles Darwin made this point in the *Descent of Man,* where he recognized the importance of give and take to human survival: "The small strength and speed of man, his want of natural weapons, etc., are more than counterbalanced by his...social qualities, which lead him to give and receive aid from his fellow-men."[2] If we value our ties to others, we must also value loneliness, which encourages us to preserve those ties.

The problem we face in today's society is that the network of shared connections has frayed so much that we do not know how we can alleviate loneliness when it takes hold. In former times, the interdependency of community life kept lonely people actively involved with others until new emotional bonds could develop. Now when we are lonely, we often need to invent our own ways to link up with others. Those whose inventiveness fails them find that loneliness becomes a chronic circumstance of their lives. Loneliness then loses its "purpose" as a motivating force and becomes instead a prison.

We offer a simple principle as an antidote: When people join together in shared tasks, unafraid of accepting and offering help, they initiate a process of give and take that extends naturally into other areas of their lives and creates fertile ground for increasing emotional depth and closeness. Such social patterns were once hard to avoid. Now these connections must be actively sought or even created anew in an increasingly fragmented and lonely world. Much of this book has offered specific advice about how that can be accomplished.

When two or more people come together to accomplish a shared task, their involvement with each other develops naturally and slowly. They come together without the forced quality so poignantly conveyed by some attempts to create relationships with strangers through personal ads or dating service videos. It is like meeting a mate in class or on the job rather than on a blind date. The process of getting to know each other happens with little self-conscious effort. Each person can get used to the other without having to plunge into emotional or physical closeness before it "feels right" or, alternately, without having to sustain a developing relationship on small talk alone.

## All Shared Tasks Are Not Alike

The phenomenon that we have described applies to love, friendship, families, and neighborhoods. It is an antidote to our increasing isolation and loneliness. In our emphasis on personal relationships, however, we have omitted important political implications of this process of give and take. The work of Harvard's Robert Putnam, whose research on civic involvement we mentioned in chapters 1 and 6, suggests that there is a link between a people's involvement in shared tasks and the vitality of a democracy.

In a recent book titled *Making Democracy Work: Civic Traditions in Modern Italy,* Putnam connects the successful development of regional governmental institutions in northern Italy to a strong tradition of civic engagement. This movement is made evident by extensive memberships in guilds, clubs, mutual aid societies, and the like. By contrast, southern Italy lacks a tradition of participation in civic organizations. Loyalty is instead centered on the family. With no shared organizations or causes uniting individuals across family lines, mutual suspicion divides families from each other; regional government is trapped in a web of mistrust, universally viewed as corrupt and ineffective.

Putnam sees the failure of government in southern Italy as the direct result of the lack of "social capital"—a resource created by networks of civic engagement and traditions of give and take which he calls "reciprocity." If he is right, then America is in trouble as well. Putnam has impressively documented a dramatic drop in the number of people participating in civic associations and other groups, from the League of Women Voters to PTAs to bowling leagues.

All shared projects are not equivalent. We can solve the problem of loneliness through shared activities with a small social group, while the society around us becomes more fragmented and mistrustful. It takes a network of social connections that extends beyond a small circle of family and friends to curb suspicion and cynicism.

A simple illustration comes up every time we talk to relatives who live in New York City about the experience of having home repairs done. Their classic "paranoid New Yorker" stance reflects the mistrust that is almost invariably present when a work contract is not, as Putnam puts it, "embedded within a larger structure of personal relations and social networks."[3] Put more simply, not only are the workmen and our relatives strangers to each other, they are not linked by any other shared concerns or social involvements. How much safer we feel when the painter's son and our own are on the same Little League team and we each care what the other says about us on the sidelines.

This commonsense conclusion fits with recent development in a branch of mathematics called game theory. In a famous conundrum called the Prisoner's Dilemma each of two prisoners is asked if the other committed a crime. Prisoner X knows that he will receive an extremely harsh punishment if he refuses to give information to the authorities while Prisoner Y does give them information. Prisoner X's punishment will be less severe if they both inform on each other. He will receive a mild punishment if they both manage to withhold information. If Prisoner X betrays Prisoner Y while Prisoner Y does not betray him, Prisoner X wins complete freedom.

The dilemma is a way to examine the conflict between individual self-interest and group well-being. The logic of game theory leads to the unsettling conclusion that the "best move" is always betrayal. Yet people, and animals for that matter, still cooperate with each other. Why hasn't Darwinian selection eliminated loyalty and altruism from the natural world?

The answer, of course, is one that Darwin himself recognized: Individuals usually remain in stable groups where they have to deal with the same people over and over again in a relationship of give and take. Computer simulations of the Prisoner's Dilemma show that simple betrayal is no longer a winning strategy when the game lasts for more than one round. Your opponent remembers your last move and it influences his next move, which is why con artists move around a lot. When our dealings with others occur outside of a stable social network, they become more like a single round of the Prisoner's Dilemma.

Not everyone is reassured by knowing their painter socially, however. Some people gravitate to cities specifically to avoid the obligations that come along with being known. Joan, a twenty-seven-year-old medical student, on the verge of moving from Boston to Ann Arbor, Michigan, talked in therapy about her antipathy for a small-town life with too many overlapping social circles.

"I don't want to live in a town where everyone knows everyone else's business," she observed. "I'm not so great with plumbers, carpenters, and people who work for me. I tend to get bitchy. I don't want to treat someone badly and then have it thrown back at me through the grapevine because the plumber told my husband's boss's wife. I love the anonymity of the big city."

Joan is a modern young woman, assertive but not to the point of abrasiveness. She simply did not want to live in a place where people are held accountable for their treatment of others, where a lack of civility can have a lasting effect on a person's reputation. Many of us are drawn to the freedom of anonymous city life, particularly during times of turmoil and transition, like leaving home for the first time or resettling after a divorce. However, the long-term price of this freedom is an erosion of trust within a community. Joan's wish to be able to treat another badly and then disappear into the anonymity of city life in fact makes her someone whom a plumber should not trust.

Realistic mistrust is an even greater problem in city neighborhoods where crime and danger have become an inescapable part of everyday life. In this environment most people are both too demoralized and too terrified to join together in a common enterprise. Even the simple shared task of mothers chatting while they watch their children play together is obliterated by isolating fear. Mothers focus instead on strategies that enable them to keep their children safely inside and apart from others.

Yet even here, where the battle for community seems most clearly lost, the danger itself can bring people together through the shared task of a crime watch or neighborhood patrol. These groups may then become the seedlings of future civic associations in the broadest sense: as people interact with each other for mutual self-protection, they begin to know each other, to develop overlapping circles of friends, to extend their involvement with each other into new areas, and perhaps to reclaim a small piece of ground in which trust and safety can grow anew.

The primary value of community participation is to create a network of connections between individuals in which trust can survive and, with it, effective democratic institutions. It trivializes a subject of immense importance to propose civic involvement solely as a self-help strategy for those who are lonely.

Putnam's research instead strongly supports the traditional view that civic participation is the essential duty of anyone who wants democracy to actually work. In our struggle with loneliness, we note that participation in local government, town music groups, local athletics leagues, or professional organizations is as good a way as any of meeting people and relieving loneliness, with the added benefit of contributing to the good of the larger community along the way.

## The Terrors of the Overscheduled Life

At this point, some of you are probably muttering to yourselves, "Just where am I supposed to find the time for all these extra shared tasks and all this community involvement? My life is already so over-scheduled that I can barely manage."

Most of the professional women we know feel that time management is the most important concern in their lives. Since women have achieved social permission to "have it all"—including children and a career—they have become accustomed to working what amounts to two jobs, one in the work place and another at home, what Berkeley sociologist Arlie Hochschild calls "the second shift."[4] As a result, they are chronically depleted and have difficulty finding joy or satisfaction in anything they do. Men also report feeling too busy and tired as they try to become more involved with their children than their own fathers were with them. Add in the "satisfaction" of mutual projects with neighbors and pretty soon there is no time left for relaxation.

Singles are as likely to schedule their lives at a frantic pace as couples. Pacing is all and it is hard to get it right. If a single person takes on too many activities, he or she can be in the absurd position of having no time available to get to know anyone in greater depth. Further, the more seriously someone takes their commitments, the more he may feel hemmed in by the projects he has taken on.

One man told us in therapy, "I am solitude-phobic. I need to be doing things with people nonstop or else I start feeling like a social failure, the way I did in high school. But this is bad because many of my interests require me to work alone. Plus, I'm always feeling guilty because I don't see enough of the friends I do have."

Fear of being alone leads many single people to overschedule their lives, but an overhectic life can generate a sense of helplessness and loneliness just as powerfully as an empty life because no time is left for relationships to deepen. As we wrote earlier, psychologist Sidney Jourard defined a deep relationship as one in which you can be yourself, talk freely with little censorship, and relax. When the deepest relationships involve sexuality, there must also be sufficient time for two people to unwind together, enough to enjoy sensual pleasure. Perhaps the curious recent phenomenon of more people complaining of decreased sexual interest stems from this tendency toward frantic overload.

Clearly if your life is overbooked, you need to occasionally prune the clutter from your schedule. John Woodward, a professor at the University of Nebraska, studied loneliness in rural Nebraska in 1987. He found that adolescents and college-age students who were involved in three to five extracurricular activities were lonelier than those who were involved in only one. With adults as well, "there was a trend for those with more activities to be lonelier."[5]

Woodward speculates that people who are lonely to start with may be more likely to seek out a greater variety of activities, but his study shows that overjoining and overscheduling is not the answer. In this book, we have presented mutual tasks and activities as a way to feel connected and anchored in a social web (the opposite of loneliness). Of course, it is certainly possible to overdo it and find that the frenetic pace of life weakens each strand in the web.

In the press of modern life, people who are intimately involved with each other must be willing to devote some time to the mutual task of learning to relax together. It may sound paradoxical to place relaxation on a busy "to-do" list, but it does take time. The trick is to appreciate that time to relax is as essential for intimacy as water, fertilizer, and sunshine are for a prize rose. If there is no time for depth in any relationship, if there is no leisure and quiet in knowing another person, then life starts to lose its savor and loneliness reemerges.

Sadly, many people complain to their therapists that they have lost the knack of relaxation and they wish to relearn it. In the 1950s, a traditional ritual of relaxation was to come home from a busy day and accelerate the unwinding process with a cocktail or a couple of beers.

Today more people expect to be able to achieve calm without chemical assistance, although exceptions are made for certain prescribed medications. We are embarrassed if we depend on any substance for our comfort and, in our American hearts, would prefer to be able to relax with a peaceful walk down a country road or a ride on the open range. Most formal nonchemical means of relaxation like yoga and meditation still feel a bit foreign or unnatural to many of us, yet we continue to need help unwinding.

Consciously experimenting with an intimate to find a way to relax together is one way to safeguard some peaceful time, but it requires a major shift in expectations. Instead of expecting that we present ourselves fully mellow and relaxed for a moment of specially planned togetherness, we would go back to depending on each other to ease the path to relaxation. The particular path chosen is a matter of shared taste, whether poetry, massages, or time in the bath, although the soothing effect of touch in particular seems built into our basic physiology.

In many other cultures, there was less need to shift gears between work and relaxation. A small leisure class claimed time for pleasure and contemplation while working people worked. Now we expect to weave both activities into our lives and often within each day. We even expect to move instantaneously from frenetic work to a laid-back mode, wasting none of our precious time on the transition. This is an absurd goal.

Living in an age of faxes and E-mail may fool us into thinking that emotions can be switched on and off easily, but they cannot. Just as it takes an extended period of time to become comfortable with someone in a relationship, relaxing with another person also takes more time and creative energy than most of us imagine.

## A Cup of Sugar

In our review of American social history, we saw how the process of give and take, once central to lives, was gradually pushed aside by a stronger commitment to making it on our own. We learned that this transformation carries with it increased loneliness, medical problems, and even shortened life spans for creatures meant to live within a social network. Furthermore, the decrease in the "social capital" once created by overlapping circles of give and take gives us reason to fear for the health of our democratic institutions. We considered the partial solution to loneliness offered by drugs, psychotherapy, and self-help groups. We then proposed specific ways to restore the process of give and take to a central position in our lives, reestablishing our connections with one another through shared tasks.

In presenting these ideas, we have had to move back and forth between the essential underpinnings provided by scholarly research and an examination of the simplest activities of our daily lives. Change, if it comes at all, must take place in the realm of the ordinary. In the midst of writing this book, one of us said to a friend, "if we could get a few people to go next door more regularly to borrow an egg or a cup of sugar, the book will be worthwhile."

When two neighbors borrow eggs from each other, they accept "grocery backup" as a shared task to avoid extra visits to the store. They gain more than just a little free time for relaxation or family, however. They draw closer to one another and begin to create a social web in the neighborhood or in an apartment building. When people remember how to lean comfortably on each other, giving and receiving favors without making a big deal of it, they are less lonely. The social web that lets each of us feel anchored and protected is woven from simple, everyday interactions that take place on a regular basis. In their absence, Durkheim's *anomie* grows. Borrowing an egg, secure in the knowledge that you will soon lend one in return, can be an act of remarkable power.

# Notes

## Chapter 1
## Our Increasing Isolation

1. *The Gallup Poll Monthly* (Mar. 1990), 31.

2. *United States Census Bureau Current Population Reports,* Series P20, No. 33 (Feb. 12, 1951) 13.

3., 4., 5. *The Lifestyle Odyssey,* Research Alert, 1992, 43; S. Rawlins, *Household and Family Characteristics,* March 1992, U.S. Dept. of Commerce, vii; R. Putnam, "Bowling Alone," *Journal of Democracy* (Jan. 1995), 73.

6. R. Putnam, "Bowling Alone," *Journal of Democracy* (Jan. 1995), 67–73.

7. S. Finn, and M. Gorr, "Social Isolation and Social Support as Correlates of Television Viewing Motivations," *Communication Research* 15 (2) (April 1988) 135–58.

8. L. Mullins, *Journal of Applied Gerontology* 10(A) (Dec. 1991), 455–68.

## Chapter 2
## The Roots of Our Fear of Dependency

1. P. Slater, *The Pursuit of Loneliness* (Boston: Beacon Press, 1970), 5.

2. Stephen Innes, *Work and Labor in Early America* (Chapel Hill: University of North Carolina Press, 1988), 3.

3. Pauline Maier, and William R. Kenan, Professor of History at MIT, personal communication.

4. Darrett and Anita Rutman, "Parental Death," in *The Chesapeake in the Seventeenth Century,* eds. Thad Tate and David Ammerman (Chapel Hill: University of North Carolina Press, 1979) 165–68.

5. Pauline Maier, personal communication.

6. Gordon S. Wood, *The Radicalism of the American Revolution* (New York: Alfred A. Knopf, 1993).

7. Pauline Maier, personal communication.

8. P. Maier, "Revolutionary Origins of the American Corporation," *William and Mary Quarterly* (Jan. 1993), 58.

9. A. deTocqueville, *Democracy in America,* ed. Phillips Bradley, 1945 (New York: A. A. Knopf, 1945 [orig. pub. 1835]), 106–107.

10. ibid., 508.

11. R. Bellah, et al., *Habits of the Heart* (New York: Harper and Row, Perennial Library, 1986), 15.

12. H. Fichtenau, *Living in the Tenth Century: Mentalities and Social Orders* (Univ. of Chicago), reprinted from the *New York Times Book Review,* Aug. 1991.

13. N. Cowan, and R. Cowan, *Our Parents' Lives,* (New York: Basic Books, 1989), 48.

14. *Science News,* Aug. 1, 1992, vol. 142, 78.

15. S. Coontz, *The Way We Never Were,* (New York: Basic Books, 1992.)

16. ibid., 45.

17. ibid., 46.

18. M. Katz, *Poverty and Policy in American History* (New York: Academic Press, 1983), 183.

19. J. M. Farragher, "Open-Country Community: Sugar Creek," Illinois, 1820–1850, in *The Countryside in the Age of Capitalistic Transformation,* ed. Steven Hahmond and Jonathn Prude (Chapel Hill: University of North Carolina Press, 1985), 245.

20. Coontz, *The Way We Never Were,* 97–98.

21. W. N. Grubb, and M. Lazerson, *Broken Promises: How Americans Fail Their Children* (New York: Basic Books, 1982), 283.

22. Coontz, *The Way We Never Were,* 97–98.

23. M. Midgely, *Can't We Make Moral Judgments?* (New York: St. Martin's Press, 1991), 120.

24. R. Bellah, et al., *Habits Of The Heart* (New York: Harper & Row, Perennial Library, 1986), 89.

25. As quoted in A. Bloom, *The Closing of the American Mind* (New York: Simon & Schuster, 1987), 62; from A. Rand, *The Fountainhead* and *The Anthem.*

26. R. Bellah, ibid., 146.

27. U.S. Census Statistics: *Household and Family Statistics,* Mar. 1992, vii.

28. *The Economist,* Oct. 16, 1993, 62.

29. S. Coontz, ibid., 178–79.

30. As quoted in *The New York Times,* July 17, 1994, E3.

31. C. Lasch, C. *The Culture of Narcissism,* 382–84.

## Chapter 3
## The Hazards of Loneliness

1. J. G. Bruhn and S. Wolf, *The Roseto Story: An Anatomy of Health.* (Norman: University of Oklahoma Press, 1979) 45–46.

2. ibid., 41.

3. B. Egolf, J. Lasker, and S. Wolf, "The Roseto effect: A 50-year comparison of mortality rates." *American Journal of Public Health* 82:1089–92, 1992.

4. S. Wolf, and J. G. Bruhn, *The Power of the Clan: The Influence of Human Relationships on Heart Disease.* New Brunswick: Transaction Publishers, 1993.

5. ibid., ix.

6. ibid., 125.

7. ibid., 122.

8. S. Cobb, "Social Support As a Moderator of Life Stress," *Psychosomatic Medicine,* 38:300–14, 1976.

9. J. Cassel, "The Contribution of the Social Environment to Host Resistance," *American Journal of Epidemiology,* 104:107–23, 1976.

10. M. Pilisuk, and S. H. Parks, *The Healing Web: Social Networks and Human Survival* (Hanover: University Press of New England, 1986), 1.

11. E. Durkheim, *Suicide: A Study in Sociology* (New York: Free Press, 1951).

12. S. Cobb, *op. cit..*

13. J. S. House, K. R. Landis, and D. Umberson, "Social Relationships and Health," *Science,* 241:540–45, 1988.

14. J. J. Lynch, *The Broken Heart: The Medical Consequences of Loneliness* (New York: Basic Books, 1977), xiii.

15. R. B. Case, A. J. Moss, N. Case, *et al,* "Living Alone After Myocardial Infarction: Impact on Prognosis," *Journal of the American Medical Association* 267:515–19, 1992.

16. R. B. Williams, J. C. Barefoot, R. M. Califf, *et al*, "Prognostic Importance of Social and Economic Resources Among Medically Treated Patients With Angiographically Documented Coronary Artery Disease." *Journal of the American Medical Association*, 267:520–24, 1992.

17. T. E.Seeman, and S. L. Syme, "Social Networks and Coronary Artery Disease: A Comparison of the Structure and Function of Social Relations as Predictors of Disease," *Psychosomatic Medicine*, 49:341–54, 1987.

18. P. D. Thomas, J. M. Goodwin, and J. S.Goodwin, "Effect of Social Support on Stress-Related Changes in Cholesterol Level, Uric Acid Level, and Immune Function in an Elderly Sample," *American Journal of Psychiatry*, 142:735–37, 1985.

19. D. Spiegel, J. R. Bloom, H. C. Kraemer, and E. Gottheil, "Effect of Psychosocial Treatment on Survival of Patients With Metastatic Breast Cancer," *Lancet* ii:888–91, 1989.

20. I. F. Fawzy, N. W. Fawzy, C. S. Hyun, *et al.*, "Malignant Melanoma: Effects of Early Structured Psychiatric Intervention, Coping, and Affective State on Recurrence and Survival Six Years Later," *Archives of General Psychiatry*, 50:681–89, 1993.

21. R. W. Bartrop, E. Luckhurst, L. Lazarus, *et al.*, "Depressed Lymphocyte Function After Bereavement," *The Lancet*, 1:834–36, 1977.

22. M. Laudenslager, M. Reite, and R. Harbeck, "Immune Status During Mother-Infant Separation," *Psychosomatic Medicine*, 44:303, 1982.

23. M. Reite, R. Harbeck, and A. Hoffman, "Altered Cellular Immune Response Following Peer Separation," *Life Sciences*, 29:1133–36, 1981.

24. J. S. House, K. R. Landis, D. Umberson, *op. cit.*.

25. S. J. Schleifer, S. E. Keller, M. Camerino, *et al.*, "Suppression of Lymphocyte Stimulation Following Bereavement," *Journal of the American Medical Association*, 250:374–77, 1983.

26. S. Jacobs, and A. Ostfeld, "An Epidemiological Review of the Mortality of Bereavement," *Psychosomatic Medicine*, 39:344–57, 1977.

27. J. K. Kiecolt-Glaser, L. D. Fisher, P. Ogrocki, *et al.*, "Marital Quality, Marital Disruption, and Immune Function," *Psychosomatic Medicine*, 49:13-32, 1987.

28. J. K. Kiecolt-Glaser, S. Kennedy, S. Malkoff, *et al.*, "Marital

Discord and Immunity in Males," *Psychosomatic Medicine*, 50:213–29, 1988.

29. J. K. Kiecolt-Glaser, W. Garner, C. Speicher, *et al.*, "Psychosocial Modifiers of Immunocompetence in Medical Students," *Psychosomatic Medicine*, 46:7–14, 1984.

30. J. W. Pennebaker, J. K. Kiecolt-Glaser, and R. Glaser, "Disclosure of Traumas and Immune Function: Health Implications for Psychotherapy," *Journal of Consulting and Clinical Psychology*, 56:239–45, 1988.

31. J. Garbarino, "The Human Ecology of Child Maltreatment: A Conceptual Model for Research," *Journal of Marriage and the Family*, 39:721–35, 1977.

32. J. Belsky, "Child Maltreatment: An Ecological Integration," *American Psychologist*, 35:320–35, 1980.

33. E. H. Newberger, R. L. Hampton, T. J. Marx, and K. M. White, "Child Abuse and Pediatric Social Illness: An Epidemiological Analysis and Ecological Reformulation," *American Journal of Orthopsychiatry*, 56:589–601, 1986.

34. P. Sainsbury, "The Epidemiology of Suicide," in *Suicide*, ed. A Roy (Baltimore: Williams and Wilkins, 1986), 17–40.

35. C. R. Roberts, R. E. Roberts, and J. M. Stevenson, "Women, Work, Social Support and Psychiatric Morbidity," *Social Psychiatry*, 17:167–73, 1982.

36. J. Bond, "Psychiatric Illness in Later Life. A Study of Prevalence in a Scottish Population," *International Journal of Geriatric Psychiatry*, 2:39–57, 1987.

37. S. A. Stansfeld, J. E. J. Gallacher, D. S. Sharp, and J. W. G. Yarnell, "Social Factors and Minor Psychiatric Disorder in Middle-Aged Men: A Validation Study and a Population Survey," *Psychological Medicine*, 21:157–67, 1991.

38. G. W. Brown and T. Harris, *Social Origins of Depression: A Study of Psychiatric Disorder in Women* (New York: Free Press, 1978).

39. C. D. Sherbourne, "The Role of Social Support and Life Stress Events in Use of Mental Health Services," *Social Science and Medicine*, 27:1393–1400, 1988.

40. R. C. Kessler, K. S. Kendler, A. Heath, *et al.*, "Social Support, Depressed Mood, and Adjustment to Stress: A Genetic Epidemiologic Investigation," *Journal of Personality and Social Psychology*, 62:257–72, 1992.

41. G. L. Klerman and M. M. Weissmann, "Interpersonal Psycho-therapy (ITP) and Drugs in the Treatment of Depression," *Phar-macopsychiatry,* 20:3–7, 1987.

42. E. Frank, D. J. Kupfer, E. F. Wagner, *et al.,* "Efficacy of Interpersonal Psychotherapy as a Maintenance Treatment of Recur-rent Depression," *Archives of General Psychiatry,* 48:1053–59, 1991.

43. M. M. Weissmann, and J. C. Markowitz, "Interpersonal Therapy: Current Status," *Archives of General Psychiatry,* 51:599–606, 1994.

44. N. Bolger and J. Eckenrode, "Social Relationships, Person-ality, and Anxiety During a Major Stressful Event," *Journal of Person-ality and Social Psychology,* 61:440–49, 1991.

45. J. S. House, K. R. Landis, and D. Umberson, *op. cit..*

## Chapter 4
## Psychotherapy: One of the Possible Cures for Loneliness

1. E. Hoffman, *Lost in Translation* (New York: E.P. Dutton, 1989) 140, 263.

2. S. Jourard, *The Transparent Self* (New York: Van Nostrand Reinhold, 1971).

3. A. Storr, *The Art of Psychotherapy* (New York: Methuen, 1979) 24–25.

4. R. Schwartz, *The Journal of Pastoral Care,* Vol. XLIII, No. 1, 42, 1989.

5. P. Kramer, *Listening to Prozac* (New York: Viking, 1993).

6. E. Schein, *Organizational Psychology* (New Jersey: Prentice-Hall, 1965) 108.

7. M. Csikszentmihalyi, *Flow: The Psychology of Optimal Experience* (New York: Harper & Row, 1990).

## Chapter 5
## Medicine, Drugs, and Loneliness

1. B. Berger, Review of *The Homeless* by C. Jencks, *New York Times Book Review,* April 24, 1994, 22.

2. J. Kagan, J. S. Reznick, C. Clarke, et. al., "Behaviorial Inhibition to the Unfamiliar," *Child Development,* 55:2212–25, 1984.

3. J. Kagan, J. S. Resnick, and N. Snidman, "Biological Bases of Childhood Shyness," *Science,* 240:167–71, 1988.

4. J. Kagan, J. S. Resnick, and J. Gibbons, "Inhibited and Uninhibited Types of Children," *Child Development,* 60:838–45, 1989.

5. R. S. Schwartz, "Mood Brighteners, Affect Tolerance, and the Blues," *Psychiatry,* 54:397–403, 1991.

6. S. Jacobs, J. C. Nelson, and S. Zisook, "Treating Depressions of Bereavement With Antidepressants," *Psychiatric Clinics of North America,* 10:501–10, 1987.

7. A. Storr, *Solitude.* (Ballantine Books, 1989), 30

8. ibid., 31

9. S. Drucker, "If I Ruled the World" (An Interview with Fran Lebowitz), *Mirabella,* November 1994, 114.

10. R. B. Aranow, R. S. Schwartz, and M. D. Sullivan, "Clinical and Ethical Issues Raised by the Development of Mood Brightening Agents," Presented at the American Psychiatric Association Annual Meeting, 1991.

11. S. D. Bacon, "Alcohol and Complex Society," In *Society, Culture, and Drinking Patterns,* eds. D.J. Pittman and C.R. Snyder, (New York: John Wiley and Sons, 1962), 87–88. (Originally presented as a lecture at the Yale Summer School of Alcohol Studies in 1944.)

12. G. E. Vaillant, *The Natural History of Alcoholism: Causes, Patterns, and Paths to Recovery.* (Cambridge: Harvard University Press, 1983), 208.

## Chapter 6
## The Small Group Phenomen

1. Robert Wuthnow, *Sharing the Journey* (New York: Free Press, 1994), 4.

2. Melinda Blau, "Recovery Fever," *New York,* September 9, 1991, 32.

3. ibid.

4. ibid.

5. Michael Brennan, "Self-Indulgent Self-Help," *Newsweek,* January 20, 1992, 8.

6. M. Blau, *op. cit.,* 35.

7. Jane Bryant Quinn, "Self-Help for the Jobless," *Newsweek,* December 16, 1991, 52.

8. Archie Brodsky, Stanton Peele, "AA Abuse," *Reason,* November 1991, 23.

9. Nicholas Lemann, "The Vogue of Childhood Misery," *Atlantic Monthly*, March 1992, 122.

10. Wendy Kaminer, *I'm Dysfunctional, You're Dysfunctional* (Reading, MA: Addison-Wesley, 1992), 13.

11. ibid., 27.

12. R. Wuthnow, *op. cit.*, 15.

13. ibid., 24.

14. ibid., 151.

15. Deborah Bebb, "Moms Helping Moms Beat Postpartum Blues," *Family Circle*, September 1, 1995, 19.

## Chapter 7
## What to Do If You Feel Single, Lonely, and Friendless

1. A. Storr, *Solitude: A Return to the Self*, (New York: Ballantine Books, 1988), xiii.

2. M. Csikszentmihalyi, *Flow: The Psychology of Optimal Experience*, Harper Perennial, 1990.

3. *New York Times Book Review*, Aug. 9, 1992, 8.

4. B. Ehrenreich, *The Worst Years of Our Lives*, Pantheon Books, 1990.

5. *Boston Globe*, April 6, 1995.

6. C.Rubenstein and P. Shaver, *In Search of Intimacy* (New York: Delacorte Press, 1982), 175.

7. ibid., 178–82.

## Chapter 8
## Single Parenthood

1. Carol M. Anderson, Ph.D., Susan Stewart, Ph.D., with Sona Dimidjian, *Flying Solo: Single Women in Midlife* (New York: W.W. Norton & Co., 1994), 253.

2. Robert S. Weiss, *Going It Alone* (New York: Basic Books, 1979), 189.

3. Alan Ebert, "Single Dads," *Good Housekeeping*, June, 1993, 130.

4. Robert S. Weiss, *Going It Alone*, 174–75.

5. ibid., 173.

6. Mildred Hope Witkin, Ph.D., with Burton Lehrenbaum, *45 and Single Again* (New York: Dembner Books, 1985), 5.

7. John Rosemond, "Raising A Child Alone: How to Escape the Single Parent Trap," *Better Homes & Gardens,* April 1992, 33.

8. Carol M. Anderson, Ph.D., Susan Stewart, Ph.D., with Sona Dimidjian, *Flying Solo: Single Women in Midlife,* 285–86.

9. ibid.

10. Robert S. Weiss, *Going It Alone,* 174.

11. Stephen L. Atlas, *The Parents Without Partners Sourcebook* (Philadelphia, PA: Running Press, 1984), 131.

12. Dawn B. Sova, *Sex and the Single Mother* (New York: Dodd, Mead & Co., 1987), 152.

13. Hojat, Mohammadreza, Wolfgang H. Vogel, "Socioemotional Bonding and Neurobiochemistry," *Loneliness: Theory, Research, and Applications.* Eds. Mohammedreza and Rick Crandall. (San Rafael, CA: Select Press, 1987), 135–44.

14. Joyce Maynard, "Sex and the Single Mom," *Redbook,* March 1993, 34.

15. Geoffrey L. Greif, *The Daddy Track and The Single Father* (Lexington, MA: D.C. Heath & Co., 1990), 95–96.

16. ibid., 103.

## Chapter 9
## Marriage and Other Long-term Commitments

1. The Editors of Research Alert, *The Lifestyle Odyssey* (Naperville, IL: Sourcebooks Trade, 1992), 44.

2. R. S. Schwartz, "Managing Closeness in Psychotherapy," *Psychotherapy,* 30:601–07, 1993.

3. G. W. Brown, and T. Harris, *Social Origins of Depression* (New York: The Free Press, 1978).

4. J. Olds, R. S. Schwartz, S. Eisen, R. W. Betcher, and A. Van Nielm "Part-time Employment and Marital Well-being: A Hypothesis and Pilot Study," *Family Therapy,* 20:1–16, 1993.

5. R. Wildavsky, "What's Behind Success in School?" *Reader's Digest,* October 1994, 49–55.

## Chapter 10
## Making Extended Families Work

1. *The New York Times,* Aug. 1, 1993, "News of the Week in Review."

2. S. Bender, *Plain and Simple: A Woman's Journey to the Amish* (San Francisco: HarperCollins, 1989).

3. ibid., 43.

4. ibid., 72–73 .

## Chapter 11
## Networking in the Neighborhood

1. Beth Daley, "Bloomfield Street's Good Neighbor," *The Boston Globe*, February 3, 1995, 27.

2. Renee Loth, "The Kindest Cut," *The Boston Globe Magazine*, December 4, 1994, 10.

3. Tovah Redwood, "Real Estate or Real Mistake?" *Michigan Today*, December 1994, 14.

4. ibid.

5. Kathryn McCamant and Charles Durrett, with Ellen Hertzmann, *Cohousing: A Contemporary Approach to Housing Ourselves* (Berkeley, CA: Ten Speed Press, 1994), 7.

6. Ray Oldenburg, *The Great Good Place* (New York: Paragon House, 1989).

7. ibid., 9.

8. ibid.

9. Alexander Reid, "Under One Roof, Several Generations," North Weekly Section, *The Boston Globe*, 1.

10. ibid.

11. ibid.

12. ibid.

13. McCamant, Durrett, and Hertzmann, *Cohousing: A Contemporary Approach to Housing Ourselves*, 12.

14. ibid., 7.

15. Amitai Etzioni, *The Spirit of Community: The Reinvention of American Society* (New York: Simon & Schuster, 1993), 125.

16. Robert D. Putnam, "Bowling Alone," *Journal of Democracy*, January, 1995, 70.

17. ibid., 71.

18. ibid., 72.

19. ibid., 69.

20. Joe Volz, "Loneliness a Stalker of Many Elderly People," *The Plain Dealer*, January 15, 1995, 10–I.

21. ibid.

22. McCamant, Durrett, and Hertzmann, *Cohousing: A Contemporary Approach to Housing Ourselves,* 12.

**Chapter 12.**
**Conclusions and Cautions**

1. R. S. Weiss, *Going It Alone: The Family Life and Social Situation of the Single Parent* (New York: Basic Books, 1979), 194.

2. C. Darwin, *Descent of Man* (Quoted in N. A. Nowak, R. M. May, and K. Sigmund, "The Arithmetics of Mutual Help," *Scientific American,* June 1995, vol. 272, 76–81.

3. R. Putnam, *Making Democracy Work: Civic Traditions in Modern Italy.* (Princeton, NJ: Princeton University Press, 1993), 172.

4. A. Hochschild with Anne Machung, *The Second Shift: Working Parents and the Revolution at Home* (New York: Viking, 1989).

5. J. Woodward, *The Solitude of Loneliness* (Lexington Books, 1988), 69–70.

# Index